Successful Stamp Dealing

Tried and Tested Tips and Techniques

Peter Mosiondz, Jr.

Published by

 **krause
publications**

700 E. State Street • Iola, WI 54990-0001
Telephone: 715/445-2214

Please call or write for our free catalog.
Our toll-free number to place an order or obtain a free catalog is 800-258-0929
or please use our regular business telephone 715-445-2214
for editorial comment and further information.

Library of Congress Catalog Number: 95-61760
ISBN: 0-87341-452-7

Printed in the United States of America

Contents

Foreword

I have had the pleasure—and it really has been that—of reading the manuscript for *Successful Stamp Dealing*. This must be the tenth or perhaps the twentieth book I have reviewed on how to succeed as a professional philatelist. And as I go back in my mind to those others, I cannot help but compare the book you hold in your hands with them.

I think other attempts have not gone back to the basics enough to see that the new dealer gets a really good start. Learning how to get a good start is sometimes best done by unlearning those things that have not been working well for you.

There are so many ways in which the dealer can lose money just paying bills. And there are dozens of tips in this book to help you get full value for everything that comes to your desk seeking money from you.

Since philately became the world's leading acquisitive hobby, dozens of books have been written on this subject. One can readily ascertain the reason. If it is so much pleasure collecting stamps, how much more desirable it would be if one made a living at it as well.

Just as styles and fashions change, so does what one needs to do and say in order to change one's approach to stamps to make it profitable. Stamp shows are different today, and advertising procedures are by no means the same. Our stamp societies now are infinitely larger, and their sales departments can offer a degree of competition previously not known. Even the use of professional mailing lists has brought changes.

Selling in clubs, at stamp shows, and with bidboards all are discussed competently here so that the new dealer may make use of them if he or she wishes. There is also a great deal about buying one's needs at auctions. Best of all in the Mosiondz book are the tips given to readers by telling many factual stories from which helpful conclusions may be taken.

All in all, it is the best book I have ever read on the subject of becoming a successful stamp dealer. If I had had the opportunity to have read such a book when I hung up my shingle six decades ago, I might have saved myself from making many costly errors.

I have enjoyed this book, and after learning some things I had not learned in sixty years as a full-time dealer, I can only wish you the same.

Herman Herst, Jr.
August 1995

Chapter 1
Getting Started

All collectors want to be stamp dealers. Or do they?

Some may think the trade is a gold-paved road leading to a spectacular personal collection, wealth, and countless free hours to enjoy the fruits. Divest yourself of that opinion. The opposite is closer to the truth.

The key word happens to be "want:" You must have the blazing inner desire to become a stamp dealer – and the need to settle only for being the best.

However, first you must have a pure love of stamps and everything philatelic. After all, the profession of selling stamps for a living is work. It's a job. And it can be a job that you love so much it is a labor of love, rather than simply labor.

This book is directed to those unfortunate souls who compose the majority of today's workforce. They hate getting up in the morning and reporting to a factory or office that they truly despise and that is filling their every day with increasingly larger doses of stress.

However, before you quit your job, be sure stamp dealing is better than what you're doing. Be sure you have a deep love for the hobby. And this passion should be laid on a foundation of integrity. If you're thinking about deceiving the uninitiated to reap huge financial gains, choose another trade.

We're a closely knit group, we stamp people. Most of us strive to conduct our affairs in an upright manner. If you deviate into illegal activities, you'll eventually be caught. Ethical dealers will be quick to point the finger at you. You also can expect a knock on your door from postal inspectors. Fraudulent use of the mails is prosecuted.

However, honesty and love for stamps also aren't enough to guarantee success. As in any other business, you must deal with events, problems, and personalities. Ideally, you should be a patient person who is highly organized and who listens carefully to others. You also should have a sincere liking for people.

A patient dealer keeps his or her cool when complaints are registered by customers. It makes no difference who's right and who's wrong. The fact is that a rude or rash reply will "turn off" your customer and can spread rapidly to other collectors.

A polite dealer is a good listener who looks directly in the eyes of customers as they speak and who never interrupts.

An organized dealer knows where to find items at the store, office, or show and also is an analytical thinker who cautiously plans every move in advance, like a chess player.

As to liking people, that's half the game. If you can't interact with others because of bias, mistrust or disaffection, then you simply cannot be a success. You might be able to "get by," but who wants that?

It also helps to avoid expressing opinions and being judgmental. Just because you don't like a particular country's stamps or a certain kind of collecting, doesn't mean that you are right and your customer is wrong. Being a successful stamp dealer means accepting others as they are. Mutual respect for each other's collecting preferences is a goal of philately generally and effective dealers specifically.

It takes years of philatelic apprenticeship to become a successful stamp dealer. And note that successful is by no means synonymous with wealthy. The apprentice period can be working for another dealer or, usually, serving under your own stewardship while you learn. You'll eat, live, breathe, and sleep stamps.

I can't stress enough how essential it is to have a working philatelic library. It's also important to follow the common advice to buy the book before the stamp. Then, all you need to do is to study the book before placing it on your shelf.

The contents of your library will vary according to the specialty you choose (more on that in the next chapter). However, some selections belong in every dealer's basic library. I can heartily recommend:

Nassau Street by Herman Herst Jr.

Foundations of Philately by Winthrop S. Boggs.

How To Detect Damaged, Altered, and Repaired Stamps by Paul W. Schmid.

Fundamentals of Philately by L.N. Williams.

Color in Philately by Roy H. White.

Where in the World? by Kenneth Wood.

This is Philately, (three volumes) by Kenneth Wood.

Post Dates: A Chronology of Intriguing Events in the Mails and Philately by Kenneth Wood.

Printing Postage Stamps by Line Engraving by James H. Baxter.

Opinions: Philatelic Expertising – An Inside View, volumes I-VI, edited by Elizabeth C. Pope for the Philatelic Foundation.

The American Philatelic Congress Books, all volumes.

The Stamp Specialist, all volumes as published by H.L. Lindquist from 1939 to 1948. These magnificent 20 volumes compose one of the most popular and informative anthologies in philatelic literature.

Scott Standard Postage Stamp Catalogue, volumes 1-5 and the *Specialized Catalogue of United States Stamps*.

Besides knowledge, you need money to start any business. Even the smallest operation needs a healthy opening balance and an adequate inventory. (The many other considerations, covered later, include stationery, advertising, printing, professional fees and equipment.)

At today's prices, a minimum of $5,000 is required for the start-up of a small, part-time mail-order stamp business. Half would go for stock, 30 percent for start-up expenses, and the final $1,000 stays in the bank for spot purchases and unexpected disbursements. You should always try to keep at least $1,000 in your checking account.

Here's a tip on getting the use of some interest-free money. With so many banks seemingly tripping over themselves to convince you to accept their Visa or MasterCard charge accounts, why not sign up for cards from two different banks? Initial credit limits can be as high as $5,000.

Here's how to use the cards to your best advantage:

We'll identify the cards as being from "Bank A" and "Bank B," each offering the hypothetical $5,000 of credit.

Using the "Bank A" card, you purchase good stock for $5,000. The bill will arrive in about a month, and you can pay it off with the $5,000 that is available to you from "Bank B." Next month you'll receive a statement from "Bank B." Now that "Bank A" is satisfied in full, you merely pay "B" with funds from "A." Repeat the process as long as necessary.

If the stock really is good, you should be able to turn it over in a month or less and in short course have made the required $5,000 profit to pay off your outstanding obligation. Most issuing banks impose an annual fee for the privilege of using their cards. However, you will have acquired some nice stock for a modest outlay. Just don't spend $10,000 at once!

Using your wits to get ahead is not the only benefit of being a stamp dealer. You also answer only to yourself for your decisions. However, if you want to succeed, you will be the hardest boss you've ever worked for.

A part-time dealer holds a steady job while dealing with stamps "on the side." His or her goal is to build the business until sales volume enables it be the owner's sole support. How much volume depends on each individual's requirements. If you're supporting a family, you'd better count on at least $100,000 in annual sales volume.

Then there are the full-time dealers whose only source of sustenance is stamp sales. I spent 14 years as a part-time stamp dealer, beginning in 1968 as a worldwide approval dealer with the barest of bare stocks and a checkbook that screamed "unfair" if an attractive buying opportunity presented itself.

An office in a spare bedroom provided the work area where I dreamed of becoming full-time. Gradually I moved on to selling just better worldwide sets, until finally I chose to deal strictly in U.S. stamps.

I was working for the day when I would knock on my boss's door and say goodbye. Imagine my shock when, without warning, I was laid-off in January 1983. Funny how the seemingly permanent things in life can turn out to be so fragile.

Then it hit me.

I had been saying for some time that I could somehow make a living from stamps with a little inventory and a pair of tongs. Now I had to prove it.

We were not financially independent. Monthly expenses were as great as anyone else's and my wife and kids liked to eat and have suitable shelter and clothing. I assured my family that there would be no problem; I was going into stamps full-time. My loved-ones looked at me as if some form of insanity had set in. But I was resolute.

You'll probably be determined, too. However, some red tape must be cleared before you hang out your "Open" sign.

There is the matter of your business name. You can use your own name or a company name.

There's a big advantage in the beginning to using your own name. You won't have to register your own name as an assumed business name. Therefore, you can continue to make deposits and withdrawals from your regular checking account. (Do be careful to properly record all income and expenses for tax purposes.) Whatever name you use you'll still have to apply at the State Sales Tax Office, unless you live in a non-sales-tax state.

The disadvantage to using your own name is that you are identifiable. You can be traced to your home by clients – and thieves. To circumvent this problem, get a post office box and unpublished phone number. If you do choose a fictitious business name, do yourself a favor. Avoid names like "Trans-Global Stamps" or "Enormous Stamp Galleries, Inc." It's useful to imply solid size, but not the impossible. Find an attractive, pleasing name. For instance, if you live in Feather Leaf Township, "Feather Leaf Stamps" would have an appealing ring.

If you decide to start out with your own name and then, if successful, change to a trade name, remember the impacts on advertising, stationery and other areas. If you think you may want to use a company name later, you might start out with it and run ads that say something like "Jimmy Jones invites you to contact Feather Leaf Stamps for prompt, courteous service." Whether you choose your own name or another, be sure to check regulations in your state about registration of business names. If you don't comply with your state's filing requirements, you place yourself in legal jeopardy.

If you indicate on your application that you will be collecting sales tax, remitting use tax or using exemption certificates, you will receive a document called something like a sales tax certificate of authority. This is the permit to collect sales tax and to use exemption certificates.

When you buy inventory for resale, you are not required to pay sales tax provided that you issue a Resale (or Exemption) Certificate to your supplier. These Resale Certificates are available from your stationer. Your obligation is to complete them factually and to enter your bonafide sales tax identification number. This number will be furnished to you by your state on your resale certificate.

If you are planning to incorporate, you must obtain a charter from your state by writing to the Corporations Division of your state's Secretary of State office. Incorporation's primary advantage is that, in the event that you are sued, your personal belongings, such as home, car, furnishings and savings, cannot be used to satisfy a judgment against you. In some situations there also are tax advantages. Your accountant can best guide you toward them.

There are also several different types of corporations. Again, your accountant can offer you the best advice for your individual needs. When inquiring, be sure to ask about potential disadvantages, as well as advantages. A limit on the salary you pay yourself is an example of one possible pitfall.

For further assistance with general business information about getting started, contact your state's small business assistance office, which probably is part of the commerce or economic development departments. Most states also offer small-business seminars, walk-in tax assistance and other services for you and your fledgling business.

Contact your nearest taxpayers' services office for more information.

If you're buying an existing business, protect yourself from becoming liable for any delinquent taxes owed by the previous owner. You must notify your state's tax division at least 10 days before sale by registered mail. State the condition of the sale, the selling price and whether or not, to your knowledge, there are any delinquent taxes due.

I once was told that the two most important friends that my business could have are my banker and my accountant. My banker told me that. A good banking relationship goes a long way in determining the success or failure of every business enterprise. Banks vary in the ways in which they treat their business clients. Some shopping around is not only important, it is absolutely necessary. Word of mouth from a business friend might be most beneficial in choosing your banker. Lacking a personal reference, there are other ways. Here's how I chose my bank.

For my business checking account, I did not want to pay high monthly service charges, per-check fees or deposit fees. I found a bank where I don't have to pay anything if I keep a minimum $500 average daily balance. Remember what I said earlier about keeping $1,000 minimum? No problem with that minimum requirement. No fees to worry about!

What I wanted most, though, was a Visa-MasterCard Merchant Deposit Account. This is an absolute necessity if you ever want to grow and generate big-ticket sales. You'll have to negotiate a commission fee with the bank. Be positive and avoid showing any uncertainty.

Proclaim that you expect your average sale to be in the $100 area. For sales in this range you will probably be able to get a 3 percent rate. This will be the commission that the bank takes on every transaction. You may or may not have to pay a monthly account maintenance fee. If you do, it probably will hover around $5 and certainly be worth every cent for the privilege of having the account.

There is a caveat when you inquire about a charge-card deposit account. Many banks will require that you have a storefront or walk-in location to qualify. Assuming that you intend to make every possible sale, you can handle walk-in traffic at your office or home. Emphasize also that you intend to accept telephone and mail sales from established accounts. To grant your bank-card deposit account, the bank probably will want to know at least half your business will be walk-in.

Banks are cautious to avoid a variety of problems. They are especially careful in protecting credit-card holders from "boiler-room" operators who use the telephone for high-pressure sales pitches (and invariably write their sales against customers' credit cards). Especially greedy phone salespeople use card numbers a second time to generate phony sales. All of this causes a hefty strain on a bank.

Keep meticulous records of your credit-card transactions. If the average ticket amount exceeds the amount that you first estimated ($100 in our hypothetical), you can go in with your evidence and renegotiate for a slightly lower rate. Keep in mind that the bank, like you, is in business to make a profit. For even the largest ticket average, you will not be able to get much lower than 1 percent. In your case, the rate will probably fall between 1.5 percent and 3 percent.

Another bank service I wanted was a business-statement savings account. I wanted to keep extra money in it, let the money earn a competitive rate of interest from the day of deposit and transfer it any time to my business checking account. I was happy to get the business-statement account.

Also ranking high on my list of banking priorities was my bank's outlook on commercial loans. When I first sat down to speak to the manager, I stipulated that my visit was solely for information. I told her I would file her response for reference. Otherwise the bank would have been obligated to report my loan inquiry to the Credit Bureau, which, in turn would record it as a customer request for a loan. This could have hampered me later if I sought an additional line of personal credit.

The manager was quick to point out that the bank had good relations with another stamp dealer and that they would be glad to consider a secured or unsecured commercial loan in keeping with my business credit needs. Of course more money would be available for borrowing if the loan were secured by collateral.

There are different kinds of collateral. However, there is one common denominator. The collateral must be tangible and liquid. The bankers favorites are real estate, stocks, bonds, certificates of deposit, and savings-account balances. Here we have definable objects with widely recognized value that a bank can liquidate easily and predictably. Some bankers also might consider items that depreciate more rapidly, like automobiles and boats.

Notice, however, that with an increase in risk to the banker comes a decrease in the amount of money that can be loaned as a percentage against collateral. To give you an example, a house with a present market value, less outstanding mortgage, of $100,000 probably will net you a loan in the neighborhood of $80,000. If you pledge your new car, new boat, and some gold bullion (which can fluctuate in value rapidly), the sum total of all three also being $100,000, you will be lucky to get $60,000. More risk or uncertainty equals less money.

This leads us to another category of possible collateral that we'll identify as the heirloom variety. Included in this group would be stamps, coins, jewelry, diamonds, artwork, and other types of collectibles. These are typically laden with many uncertainties about future value because of collector demands and fads. Heirloom collateral also is subject to wide market fluctuations and to different interpretation of value from one dealer to the next.

Liquidity is another important factor. Sale at public auction often brings the most desirable results to the owner of collectible property. Using auctions also can mean waiting months for the final settlement from the time that the property is consigned. Bankers dislike long settlement times. Their business depends on rapid turnover.

In general, small business owners must personally guarantee bank loans. Since, in most cases, your home, or more specifically the equity in it, is your single most valuable asset, guard it with care. I suggest you offer cash or securities to your banker. Safeguard the well-being of your family by leaving your home unencumbered. In general, borrow only what you can afford to lose and are able to repay, albeit over a period of time, and you'll avoid sleepless nights.

Once you have secured the loan, you will need to set up a repayment timetable with your banker. Bank loans, other than for home equity, usually run from three to five years. The longer the loan, the higher the interest rate. If you need longer payment terms, or if your banker is not completely sold on the idea of loaning you the money you need, perhaps the Small Business Administration can help you. It will guarantee up to 90 percent of the loan to a maximum of $750,000. It also can also arrange maturity dates of up to seven years for capital, 25 years for real estate.

Be sure to include these elements in a presentation for your banker:

Start with a letter of introduction. Show your business background, if any. Provide a history of your stamp business, if any. Explain your expertise with stamps in language a novice can understand.

List personal, credit and business references complete with addresses and phone numbers.

Explain why you want the money that you are requesting and how you will use it.

Include your prior-year tax return.

Include financial statements for the two previous years.
Demonstrate your ability to repay the loan.
Complete the bank's loan-application form and include it.
Package everything in a clean, businesslike presentation folder.

As a matter of practice after you secure the loan, send your banker a copy of each financial statement as soon as it is prepared. You'll not only be keeping your bank informed of your progress and rate of growth, but — most importantly — you will be creating an image of professionalism.

At this point, if you don't already have a good certified public accountant, get one. Remember, he or she will be the other of your two most important business friends. There are many useful things a CPA can do for you, including your all-important federal tax return.

One function he can perform for you right away will be your bank presentation. If you do it by yourself, it easily can appear amateurish. Your banker will notice that right away. Your accountant will speak the bank's language and increase your chance for that loan.

In your bank presentation, you'll want to include a "ratio sheet" to give the banker a quick overview of your business and to highlight the current ratio of your company's assets to liabilities. This tells the bank if you have the ability to repay the loan and how much working capital you have. Other important ratios are debt to equity and sales-to-accounts receivable. Your inventory ratio will tell your banker how quickly you turn over your stock and if you're carrying too much dead stock.

A stamp dealer should not become his or her own accountant anymore than a dentist should drill his own teeth. Depending on your needs, you can expect to pay $600 and up a year. It will be money well invested in your business success. A friend of mine spends $275 a month for his CPA's retainer for these services.

To save some money, you can perform basic accounting chores like making routine entries in your books and preparing your own monthly statements. Your accountant may suggest this himself as he shows you exactly how to set up and maintain your books.

A simple set of books consists of four journals and one ledger. The sales journal is used to record sales of merchandise. The purchase journal is used to record purchases of merchandise. The cash journal is used to record cash receipts and cash payments. The general journal is for all entries that are not made in other journals. In the ledger there is one page for each record, or account. Some accounts are cash, merchandise inventory, merchandise sales, merchandise purchases, expenses, proprietor's investment (equity), furniture, notes receivable, and notes payable.

There also should be a separate page for each customer and one for each creditor. The bookkeeper's (your) work consists of recording transactions in the proper journal as they occur and then posting (copying) these entries to their respective accounts (pages) in the ledger.

At month's end, each account's balance in the ledger is obtained and listed on a statement called the trial balance. At the end of the year (or quarter or six-month period, if you choose) a balance sheet is prepared from the trial balance to show all the assets the business owns, such as cash, merchandise inventory, customer's balances, notes receivable and the like. The business's debts (liabilities) also are listed. They include notes payable, creditor's balances, etc. The difference between the assets and the liabilities represents your net worth, or equity. By comparing net worth with net worth from the previous accounting period, you can tell whether the value of your business is increasing or decreasing.

To keep your finger on the pulse of your business, it is wise to prepare an income statement each month that shows whether you had a profit or loss for the period. An income statement simply is a list of your revenues less your expenses for the month. If revenues are larger, you have a profit. If expenses are larger you have a loss.

If you do these elementary chores yourself and rely on your accountant to do just the loan presentations, ratio sheets, the periodic financial statements and required tax returns, you could keep your annual accounting fees down to about $600, or a $50 item a month. That's quite a savings on the $275 a month that my friend pays.

Take less than two months of your savings and invest $325 in something really worthwhile and essential — a year's dues in the American Stamp Dealers' Association (ASDA). I waited too long to begin taking advantage of all the benefits of membership. It wasn't until I was in business 15 years (one of which was full-time) that I finally applied. At first I thought ASDA was necessary for only big dealers or those in New York. That's not the case at all, however. ASDA benefits all dealers.

Membership is a privilege extended to those persons deemed worthy; it is not a right. It is not as simple as paying one's dues. Every applicant is scrutinized very carefully. The bottom line is that the granting of membership is cause to celebrate. The ASDA member is strictly bound by a Code of Ethics, and failure to abide by the code is grounds for expulsion.

ASDA members include retail and wholesale stamp dealers, auction houses, supply manufacturers, jobbers, philatelic publishers and others. ASDA studies local and national legislation and rulings that relate to the philatelic field, and publishes them, when necessary, with commentary. In many instances the association has been successful in securing the reversal of rulings that were detrimental to the stamp business, and it works closely with various authorities to protect the trade.

Members receive a membership plaque and decal for office or window. Logos are supplied for your stationery and advertising, which simplifies doing business through the mail because other dealers know you as a fellow ASDA member. This enhances your credit standing in the trade. Astute collectors also prefer to do their serious business with ASDA members. ASDA also has local chapters and produces large shows known as Postage Stamp Mega-Events throughout the country each year. Two are in New York City.

In short, the aims of the American Stamp Dealers' Association are your goals: to promote stamp collecting, and thus to enlarge the stamp trade, and to keep stamp traders up-to-date in all phases of the hobby. At the same time, ASDA acts as a clearing house and coordinator of dealer efforts. Some of the benefits and services include:

ARBITRATION — Complaints of members against members are adjudicated by arbitration through the American Arbitration Association with the sole aim of settling the dispute amicably, without resorting to costly legal measures.

BUSINESS FORMS — Specialized forms for the stamp trade are available from the National Office.

COLLECTION SERVICE — Members use the services of two collection agencies at a discounted rate.

COMPLAINT BUREAU — The National Office maintains files that contain information on dealers, collectors and others who do not live up to the Code of Ethics.

CREDIT INFORMATION — Confidential credit information is available to members on collectors and dealers.

DISCOUNTS — Trade discounts with participating rental car agencies, hotels, and airlines. These are especially useful when traveling across the country attending stamp shows.

EXPERTISING SERVICE — Members may have their material expertised at a discounted rate.

IFSDA — You automatically become a member of the International Federation of Stamp Dealers Associations and you'll be given an ID card along with a copy of its annual handbook, which includes a directory of dealers worldwide (yourself included). You'll also receive its informative quarterly newsletter.

STAMP INSURANCE — All-risk, low-cost coverage is available for your entire stock.

THEFT — ASDA maintains and provides information on stolen collections and dealers' stocks.

MEMBERSHIP DIRECTORY — Members receive free of charge the annual membership directory, which contains the names, addresses and phone numbers of all members plus a description of that member's area of specialization.

NEWSLETTER — A very useful monthly publication containing current news relating to the trade. It also has a dealer-to-dealer trade page and show schedule.

In addition, numerous committees function on such matters as advertising, public relations, expertising, finance, insurance, ethics, membership and shows, to name just a few.

Without a doubt, ASDA membership is a prerequisite to becoming a successful stamp dealer. It would be my personal privilege to act as a sponsor for any dealer who wishes to join our august body.

Chapter 2
Select Your Field

Once, cities all over the nation boasted several stamp stores in the same town. Larger cities even had handfuls of stamp dealers on the same street. How times have changed! The retail store is becoming extinct now. It's not because people are losing interest in stamps. Economic factors are the villains.

Escalating expenses, especially rents, in the downtowns make it cost prohibitive for merchants to do business there unless they have fantastic turnovers of inventory or sell high mark-up or individually-high-priced big-ticket items. Stamp dealers fit neither of these descriptions. Dealers are caretakers for Lady Philately whose stamps often sit in inventory for years waiting for the right collectors.

Dealer markups can be low, too. Often dealers buy at auctions in competition with their own customers. As to big-ticket stamps or covers, it will become painfully obvious to beginning dealers that these usually are purchased only from other dealers, who add their own markups, or at auction.

Another reality is that dealers no longer can afford to carry comprehensive showings of worldwide new issues. The philatelic press reports that the total face value of all new issues of the world has been averaging more than $10,000 a year for the last decade. That's $1 million a decade a worldwide dealer could spend on *10 copies* of each new issue alone!

Today's word is specialize. You must specialize almost immediately, or the cost of your inventory will crush you. We'll get into the pros and cons of retail store, office, bourse and mail-order in the next chapter.

Specialization can be by region, country or topic. And topics can be well worth considering. You might be surprised at the many collectors interested in topical stamps because they can't afford to collect the world, or even a single country or two, anymore.

Thematic collecting also is fun, which is what I believe collecting is all about. I know two of my own favorite collections, Sherlock Holmes and World War II, attract me simply because they are enjoyable. As a dealer, I can sell topicals without having as large an investment in inventory. Most topicalists make their own album pages or use stockbooks, which diminishes the demand for a wide line of albums. Topical collectors also look for new stamps in their specialties, rather than requiring me to have most of the stamps ever issued for every country I sell.

When you make your final decision, select your specialty based on the demand for it, whether the value of its stamps is likely to rise or fall over the long run, and the number of dealers already involved in it. Let's say, for example, that demand for Vatican stamps, and consequently increasing value of them, is stagnant from your personal observations and from discussions with other stamp dealers. It probably would be a poor business decision to lay in a deep stock of Vatican stamps and to become one more dealer in a crowded field.

However, you might notice that hardly any dealers are offering postal history, cancellations, and commercial covers of the Vatican and that there is demand from specialists and advanced collectors for such material. You might want to consider this non-stamp area as your specialty.

Wait a minute, though. Specializing in Vatican covers and cancels alone will not pay the rent. Now you consider natural tie-ins of similar material. Some examples are Italy, Italian States, San Marino, Trieste, and the Allied Military Government. Stamps also can be added later.

Once you are recognized as a specialist in an area, it will open doors for your stamp sales. Customers will come to you, instead of your competitors, because of your reputation. If you had decided to go solely with Vatican stamps at first, you probably never would have become a competitor yourself because there wouldn't have been enough business in a crowded field for you to create a place for yourself.

As you may expect, how one views the competition is usually based on how one is faring. Besieged with collectors at his bourse table, a dealer may proclaim that he doesn't worry at all about his competition. He may even refer to other dealers as colleagues. Sales are good, and there's no shortage of new material. There's plenty for everyone.

Then, watch what happens when there's a lull, and it seems like an eternity since anything remotely resembling a collection was offered for sale. This same happy-go-lucky dealer starts complaining that everybody is out to get him. Suddenly, other dealers are stealing his regular customers. The bourse chairman intentionally gave him a bad table because of some imagined prejudice. Now there are too many dealers, too many shows. Complain, complain, complain.

Get used to it. This dramatic change in personality could happen to you — if you let it. Instead, take positive action when business is slow. Increase sales by discounting slow-moving material, by offering your regulars a special sale, and by other similar techniques. You can also look to auctions as an outlet for some of your wares, in addition to being important avenues to buying opportunities. Veteran dealers know that slow selling periods translate into good buying times.

Once you have chosen your specialty and feel comfortable with it, you can further subdivide it into classic or modern (20th century) postal history. Or you may want to go for both. Whatever you do, choose carefully; your philatelic livelihood depends on it.

In my case, I began as a worldwide approval dealer. I also had pet countries that I went heavily on and for which I even stocked some new issues that I had to mark up only 25% over face to stay competitive. I soon saw the folly of working on so low a profit and eventually I branched out as a U.S., Western Europe and British Commonwealth mail-order dealer.

Within a few months I made a startling discovery. Trying to be active in U.S. issues, plus the other two broad regions, was foolhardy. I soon sent the British and Europe to auction and used the proceeds to expand my U.S. stock. It's a decision I've always been comfortable with. Recently, I decided to stock only commemorative year sets for those issues from 1940 to date.

After doing some research on turnover and profit-to-cost ratios I had no choice in dropping individual U.S. stamps after 1940. These later issues, which were universally available for just over face value, were simply not worth keeping. Instead of helping to pay the rent, they were eating into my profits. There just wasn't enough markup in them.

Is there an easy way to test the philatelic marketplace? Yes, there is! Can you tell beforehand what it is that collectors really want? Yes, you can!

A relatively simple method requires membership in the American Philatelic Society. Merely check the "We Need" section in the monthly Sales Talk column in *The American Philatelist*. The APS has more than 50,000 members, many of whom request and order from the sale circuits that it distributes. These circuits are made up by its members and generate in excess of $2 million in sales every year. Naturally, the in-demand items will not have enough sales books to meet these needs. These countries, regions or topicals will appear monthly in the "We Need" column with a plea for more material.

Conversely, the items presently out of philatelic favor will be listed in the "Overstocked" column. Those listed have too much supply for too little demand. There are many other advantages to being an APS member. Actually no dealer can afford not to belong. The many benefits would fill a small booklet. The first is the sales division, which is an excellent way to dispose of slow-moving inventory if you price it right.

Next comes the American Philatelic Research Library, where you can find just the right volumes to further your research and enhance your knowledge of your specialty.

The APS/ASDA Stamp Dealer Insurance Plan offers complete protection for an unbelievably low cost. You can even have up to $50,000 worth of protection without needing a safe. You can get a low-cost rider to protect your mail shipments, too. That will allow you to use Certified Mail without the return receipt. Compare this to the cost of postal insurance. Even if you send just a few pieces a week, it could save you money. Information about insurance and other APS benefits can be obtained from the society by writing to the APS at P.O. Box 8000, State College, PA 16803.

Another way to check on current popularity of material is to study the wanted-to-buy ads in the weekly philatelic press. Obviously the U.S. material will dominate. However, you still can tell which singles and sets are in high demand. Everyone wants them!

The rest of the buy ads also tell a story. Are increasing numbers of dealers looking to buy France? Do you also see more ads lately offering France for sale? If so, you can bet that the demand for France is up.

Checking demand includes spending time at the local bourses. Note the type of material being offered. Bourses paint a local image. Nevertheless, take them into consideration. Expect German material in Milwaukee and Polish material in Chicago. What else do you see for sale? If five dealers out of the 20 have good Canadian stock and you see collectors sitting at their tables with want lists in hand, you can be sure that interest in Canada is on the upswing. And you can also bet that this interest is not purely local.

I mentioned the buy ads. You also can benefit by paying attention to the display ads that offer stamps for sale. Do you see the same advertisers week after week offering the same countries? These dealers are not philanthropists. They continue to buy advertising space because their ads get results.

Whatever decision you make on your specialty, you'll be catering to collectors. Sure investor money is nice. However, a big-spending investor may decide to pull out quickly, and you'll be hunting for customers to replace him or her. Investors also spend irregularly. You could sell $1,000 one day and go months before an investor comes to you again, if at all. Investors also seek higher priced items, the ones that are usually out of reach for the newer dealer. Collectors, on the other hand, can be just what a beginning dealer needs. They spend in smaller doses and are steady and faithful.

Earlier I mentioned my interest in World War II. While it is a fascinating area to collect that comes with a seemingly never-ending flow of material to chase, it is not the type of specialty for a fledgling dealer to choose as a sole source of income.

A narrow specialty like World War II can be added to a primary specialty though to increase your share of the market. If you specialize in the German area, for instance, seriously consider adding World War II. It's a natural revenue booster.

A prerequisite to announcing yourself as a specialist dealer is to join your field's society. The thematic dealer would automatically join the American Topical Association and the appropriate study group(s). In addition, a sports-on-stamps dealer would also join Sports Philatelists International, which is APS Affiliate 39.

There is no reason not to join as many collector societies as possible. Too many dealers brag about being members of ASDA and APS and leave it at that. The specialist societies need your support if they are to continue informing and nourishing your customers. And support is more than merely paying one's membership dues. There is advertising to be purchased in journals, recruiting to be done, and other tasks that cry out for active participation. What type of image do you want to project? Become involved.

While on the topic of support, subscribe to all of the philatelic weeklies, plus *The Stamp Wholesaler*. Advertise as well, even if they're only classified ads. It costs so little to reinvest in the hobby that treats you so well.

The United States dealer should join the Bureau Issues Association. For information contact George V.H. Godin, P.O. Box 23707, Belleville, IL 62223.

Other US related societies include:

Modern Postal History Society, c/o Ken Schoolmeester, P.O. Box

8465, Greensboro, NC 27419.

Postal History Society, c/o W. Danforth Walker, General Delivery, Lisbon, MD 21765.

Precancel Stamp Society, Paul Rosenberg, P.O. Box 129, Accord, MA 02061.

American Revenue Association, c/o Richard A. Friedberg, 310 Chestnut St., Meadville, PA 16355.

U.S. Cancellation Club, c/o Eugene Schrier, P.O. Box 815, Upper Montclair, NJ 07043.

U.S. Philatelic Classics Society, c/o Wilson Hulme, P.O. Box 5368, Naperville, IL 60567-5368.

U.S. Possessions Philatelic Society, c/o Geoffrey Brewster, 141 Lyford Drive, Tiburon, CA 94920.

Dealers will also find advantages in joining the Collectors Club of New York, even if they don't live within travel time of the clubhouse. The club's high-quality journal is second to none, and the organization has an incredible library. Contact it at 22 E. 35th St., New York, NY 10016.

The Philatelic Foundation deserves your attention as well. Its informative bulletins on fakes are especially worthwhile. There isn't a membership in the usual sense; you become a contributor to receive mailings and qualify for a discount on the expertising service, which is recognized around the world. Contact the Foundation at 501 Fifth Ave., Room 1901, New York, NY 10017. If you're traveling to New York, it is just up the street from the Collectors Club.

Education is an ongoing process. There never will be a time when you will "know it all." Seek out the specialist societies and study groups in your chosen field. Join as many as you can find.

Once you have chosen your specialty and joined philatelic societies, you can plan your business stationery. You don't want to proclaim your society memberships on your stationery until you have been formally accepted by the groups. It would be bad philatelic manners and unethical to jump the gun.

Patience is required on some of your applications, especially those to ASDA and APS. It takes time to contact your personal, business and banking references and then for your application to go to the proper committees and boards of directors. You must meet rigid standards for membership approval, especially in ASDA and APS. With this in mind, expect a wait of up to two months in most cases.

As for the actual stationery, you won't need purebreds — a few solid workhorses will do. In my business, the 5½ x8½-inch notehead and 4x6-inch postcard do the lion's share of the work when I answer day-to-day correspondence. My notehead carries the ASDA triangle in the lower right corner, the APS seal appears at the lower left, and my italicized *DEALING IN QUALITY U.S. STAMPS* is centered between both. The upper left corner is dominated by my logo "If It's U.S. Stamps, Pete can't be beat" which is stamplike in format.

There was a time when I listed all my society memberships on the notehead. After joining so many groups, however, there just wasn't room. I do list as many of the larger groups that will fit just below the name, address and logo portion at the top and run horizontally between two solid lines.

The result is an uncluttered notehead that regulates the length of my replies. If I were using a regular letterhead, I might be typing all day. I can be long-winded when my favorite subject of stamps arises.

I use an unruled 4x6-inch index card for my postcard. It's size also limits my reply to a few lines. Postcards are used whenever a short reply will do and a postal savings can be achieved. I find that business cards are a waste of money unless you work many bourses or have a walk-in location.

Your letterhead has an important place in your office and should be typeset by an established printer to appear reliable and professional to your customers. Go with a strictly uncluttered look here, with name, address, phone number and ASDA/APS logos if you're a member. At the top place a brief line indicating your specialty.

An example of the way you may use letterhead is a letter I sent to the manager of a bank that just opened an office nearby. I introduced myself as a professional philatelist who would be interested in, and capable of, performing philatelic appraisals. The image my letterhead gave the banker can influence him to send me appraisal business.

I have another 5½ x8½-inch form that does double duty. I use the form for the receipts sent to my customers and can list up to 17 items on them. I also send them out as order blanks when I do price list mailings.

To conclude our summary of workhorse stationery, let's consider the envelope. You'll want a matching printed No.10 envelope for your letterhead. Other than that, a No. 6¾ for your noteheads will suffice, with a rubber-stamped return address being used by some dealers. Others opt for the more business-like image of a printed corner card. Approval dealers also will want No. 6¼ return envelopes, as will dealers mailing price lists or mail-bid-sale listings.

Return envelopes for customer convenience can be expensive luxuries for your business. They also can increase your business by getting extra orders and causing people to return items like approvals more promptly. You may want to experiment to see which works better for you.

There is no way that I can accurately advise each reader on a starting quantity for the various pieces of stationery. In the beginning, you might consider 500 of each with your reorder figures being based on actual usage. Much of the price in commercial printing involves time for set-up, and printing additional amounts costs very little. On the other hand, capital is important for all dealers. You want to avoid tying up your money in stationery that might take several years to use. Six months to a year's worth at a time probably is enough.

Now that you have chosen a specialty, joined professional associations and collector societies and have had a supply of stationery printed, you're about ready to begin using it.

Chapter 3
Who Am I?

You've made great strides so far! But you still have an important decision to make. Are you going to open a retail store or office, work shows, or concentrate on being a mail-order dealer? Or will it be some happy combination? Who are you?

When I decided to turn my pastime into my livelihood, I had no idea I would be opening a store so early in my full-time philatelic career. I planned to work out of my home doing mail order and shows. I had a spacious office that was conveniently detached from the hustle and bustle of an exuberant household and that was in a tranquil country setting. Everything seemed ideal. However, I soon realized there are certain advantages to having a store that convinced me to set up shop.

First, I felt that collectors would feel secure dealing with me because I would be a community fixture. I could cultivate and maintain a customer base for sales. A retail location would be an even bigger benefit for buying, however. Often a collector needs to sell for instant cash. The store owner reaps the harvest.

The number of collections that had been offered to me through the mail could be counted on the fingers of one hand, with some to spare. Collectors often fear their valuable stamps will be lost in shipping or that there will be some missing items if the collection is returned when they decline a dealer's offer. If you plan to be a mail-order dealer, also plan on a lot of missionary work to persuade collectors that you are above reproach when you advertise to buy collections. You still will not get many offers. Note that when I say collections I am referring to important collections with top notch material, not the common type of material that one sees in the classified ads under the Wanted-To-Buy category.

A store also can help you sell supplies, literature and job lots, all of which are difficult to sell through the mail unless you are a recognized specialist in such material. The many discount supply dealers in the philatelic press make it tougher to sell those items in your store. However, you'll still sell enough of them to pay a few small bills. And with some imagination you may do quite well.

I had one idea that caught fire with my regular customers. My 10-and-20 Club offered them an opportunity to save money on mount purchases. I decided to handle only the most popular mounts, those most often requested, and so settled on Showgard and Hawid. I offered a 10 percent discount on a purchase of 10 assorted packs, with a 20 percent discount on 20 packs. Sales boomed!

I soon incorporated the basics of this idea with my other supply products. To give you one example, the purchaser of a $49.95 Scott National Album received a 20 percent discount off a sale of stamps equal to the album price. So the happy collector bought $50 worth of stamps to add to that brand new album and received a $10 discount on the stamp sale. Everyone was happy. I had my full profit on the album ($20) and sold stamps to boot, making an additional profit there. My customer got what amounted to a 10 percent discount on her or his entire purchase.

There are unlimited possibilities to move supplies in your store. With an eye-catching window display and some local advertising, you can bring some needed converts to Lady Philately's fold. In my case, as a U.S. dealer, I surrounded my display of commemorative year sets with various albums. Naturally, I pointed out the ridiculously low price that these stamps of the past 50 years could be obtained for when purchased on my Instant Collection Plan. Once, I even invited myself on a local radio show. I talked stamps for 30 minutes, fielded questions, and ended up with many new customers.

There also are disadvantages to stores. You'll have to pay particular attention to your hours, especially if you want to continue doing appraisals and shows. You can only be one place at a time, and you won't be able to afford professional help at first.

Fortunate indeed is the dealer who has a willing spouse. My wife bailed me out often when a bourse conflicted with my store hours. I took most of the U.S. stock with me to the bourse. There was no problem with my store regulars because I posted notices about the bourses and implied that my better stock would accompany me there. I took all my early stock and split the 20th century stock, leaving behind all the heavier material. I packed some covers to finish off my "traveling stock." Everything was light and compact. It worked! Income was generated from two sources.

If you want a mail-order business in addition to bourses, appraisals, and the like, you must provide ample time. There is no need for anyone in a retail stamp store to be open seven days a week. Depending on your locale, you can decide on three to five days and still satisfy most of your clientele. Throw in one or two nights for extended days and plan a bid-board for one of them.

Normally a bid-board would be held open for about three weeks. I always felt it to be better to have a streamlined bid-board and close it every week. This action ensures a steady traffic flow once a week. Instead of having the wall-to-wall type of board that seemed to stretch around every stamp store I visited, I decided on a 48-item display and chose to have only the more expensive items up for bid. Seldom did anything appear for under $20.

My bid-board cards recorded a code number for the owner (consignor) of the lot, a written description of catalog number, and grade. On the right-hand side, I repeated that data along with two columns for bidder number and bid on an attached coupon. The starting bid was shown on line 1. Next to the bid-board was posted an easy to understand set of instructions with proper bidding intervals. A separate hard-cover copybook contained the bidder and consignor numbers starting with 100. Names, addresses and phone numbers were duly recorded so that it was not too difficult to see who a number represented.

Every week thousands of dollars worth of material went up, and the bid-board was a huge success. Payment was prompt, too. On closing night, two lines formed, one for buyers picking up and paying for their new lots and the other for consignors receiving their money. This even-handed policy also ensured a steady stream of fresh material for consignment. Happy consignors were steady consignors. And since my commission was a straight 20 percent from the seller, I made quite a bit of extra income.

When it finally came time to decide whether I wanted a store, I explored all possibilities. Finally, I chose a mini-mall location. All this meant was that it was one step up from, and cleaner than, a flea market. Initially I had Friday, Saturday and Sunday hours, with Sunday being the only night closed. Eventually, this was expanded by the mall management to include Thursday all day and night, which increased my 30-hour schedule to 41 hours. There never were any complaints about my not being open Monday, Tuesday, or Wednesday. I had the luxury those three days of attending to other philatelic matters, including filling all those wonderful mail orders.

Before I signed the lease though, there were some important matters to address. First, was the location suitable? Sitting in my car and counting the number of vehicles coming in the single entrance to the parking lot yielded some encouraging numbers. By going inside on different days, I checked the buying habits of the patrons. This survey also offered promise. However, there was more to it than customers who spent money. The building itself had to be clean and attractive. The merchants had to look and act like professionals.

Finally, I wanted to interview management. To what extent would they serve the shopkeepers? Were they attentive to retailers' needs? Would these needs be satisfied? What about a short-term lease to give the location a try? The answers were favorable and within a few days my store opened.

I had no idea what supplies to stock; so I called my favorite jobber. I got lots of advice — all of which later proved to be accurate and reliable. Not only was I advised what to stock, I was told at what levels to maintain that stock. A reorder system was set up for mounts, stockbooks and albums.

I also learned what NOT to carry and what to avoid stocking until sufficient demand warranted it. How reassuring it was to have a philatelic pro in my corner. The day after the conversation, the UPS truck arrived with everything that I ordered, along with complimentary displays and handouts.

I got busy organizing the stamps, checking prices and worrying about everything I was sure I had forgotten. A sleepless night resulted as anticipation set in.

Then I opened the doors. What a thrill! Customers came in steadily. The flurry of buying and selling exceeded my wildest dreams. Selling from my home was nothing compared with this!

However, a store may not be your answer. Not everyone is conditioned to be the proprietor of a retail stamp store. It takes mountains of patience to spend an hour or so with a customer for a $2 sale. Your locale also may not be suited to a walk-in stamp store.

You also could discover you are your own worst enemy. I still believe I steered too many of my regulars to auctions as I talked about their virtues in print and over the counter. Auctions always will be good sources of scarce material.

However, a few years ago, I began to notice more and more mail sales that offered lower-price material to bidders without the certainty floor auctions provide that one actually has competed in a fair bidding process. Soon even sets of perforated National Parks were in these sales. And I had introduced my customers to opportunities to snap up these popular sets at prices significantly lower than I was able to offer with my overhead.

In August 1984, just a year after opening the store, I moved to an office in a professional building. I faced the prospect of going through another disastrous Christmas season at the mini-mall when all the stores were forced to stay open from the day after Thanksgiving until the end of the day on Christmas Eve. We were all assessed proportionately higher rent. I'm sure the shopkeepers with gift merchandise did very well; I did not. I sold some supplies. However, stamp sales suffered as collectors channeled their finances other places.

In the office, I concentrated my attention on expanding my mail-order business and on re-introducing my own mail-bid sales. I also was able to shorten my hours, much to the delight of my family. The gamble paid off. Not only did I cut my overhead dramatically, but I also increased my sales volume. This added up to bigger profits. I was now able to become more competitive and to recapture some customers lost to mail sales.

GROSS SALES

1982		1983		1984	
JAN-JUN	JUL-DEC	JAN-JUN	JUL-DEC	JAN-JUN	JUL-DEC
$22,742	$28,635	$33,140	$45,831	$47,296	$69,356

All of 1982 and Jan.-June of 1983 are gross sales from mail order and shows combined (I don't have specific breakdowns available as to how much was mail and how much was show).

July-Dec. of 1983 and Jan.-June of 1984 are gross sales from store, mail order, and shows. Again, no breakdowns available.

July-Dec. of 1985 are gross sales from office, mail order, and shows. No breakdown available.

Full-time stamp dealing began in January 1983.

Monthly rent for the store was $400 if memory serves correctly. The office rent was a mere $225. These figures include heat and electricity. All other expenses stayed virtually the same. There was no difference in cost of phone, travel, stationery, etc.

Comparable salaries of the period are approximately $15,000 for 1982; $16,000 for 1983; and $18,000 for 1984. Prior to getting laid-off after Christmas, 1982 (just prior to going full-time), I was earning $26,000 as a vice-president (sales and marketing).

As to the profits, I keep tax records for seven years and then discard. I have no data on these years. I can tell you that the second half of 1984 (office) compared to the second half of 1983 (store) showed an increase of over 50% in gross receipts. Meanwhile my overhead was reduced almost 44% (rent from $400 to $225). I am sure that my profits were slightly better (percentage-wise) due to the lower overhead ratio. I felt that the $175 monthly savings were not sufficient to alter my mark-ons, therefore my prices basically stayed the same.

A fringe benefit I didn't anticipate was that in my professional office building I would be able to do some prospecting for affluent clients. I circulated a flier to my new neighbors. In recognition of the fact that their hours were similar to mine, I offered an after-hours get acquainted night, complete with wine and cheese. It paid off handsomely.

The office also allowed me to devote more time to the weekend bourses. I was now setting my own hours, instead of being locked in to a schedule imposed by the mall management. Before you decide on a store look into the benefits of an office. Compare the pros and cons.

Whether you open a store, rent an office, or operate out of your home, security is the watchword. What I did and what I recommend that you do is select at least three firms that are listed in your phone directory under Burglar Alarm Systems. Look for experience. Has the company served your community for a lengthy time? Call the Better Business Bureau. Are there any complaints on file? If so, what are the allegations? Have they ever been under any investigation? How long have they been a member? These and other questions must be asked.

A licensed, bonded, and insured firm that provides references upon request and that offers nothing other than Underwriters Laboratories-approved equipment is absolutely required. Remove from your consideration any company that fails to meet any of your pre-set criteria. You want a firm that offers 24-hour emergency service and that offers at least a two-year guaranty on its installations. The equipment might carry a different guaranty or warranty from the manufacturer. Inquire about a service contract or insurance on any equipment that does not have the two-year protection.

Have your chosen firms visit you for a free estimate and consultation. Samples should be brought for demonstration and your evaluation. A professional firm will offer these services gratis. If one of your choices does not offer this "shop-at-home" service, don't waste any more of your valuable time by even considering it.

Other good features to shop for when choosing an alarm company and their system include: 24-hour central station monitoring; police response; upgrade capability as new technology or needs present themselves; passive infra-red; hold-up alarm; and fire and smoke control. Ask your candidates to explain each point.

Finally, just as stamp dealers belong to professional organizations, so do alarm dealers. Many will be members of the National Burglar & Fire Alarm Association, as well as of state chapters. Look for professional societies when inquiring about references.

If you are mechanically and electrically adept and want to save a nice chunk of money, then consider the do-it-yourself approach. Some firms will provide step-by-step instructions, demonstrations, technical assistance, systems layout, and even training.

Something else that should occupy your thoughts is a safe. Some people rush out to buy a safe thinking that they are finally secure. Just because you've spent a few hundred dollars and have a cute steel box weighing 200 pounds doesn't mean anything. Does it surprise you to learn that most burglars, amateur or professional, can enter most safes at will?

I said most. There is one safe that most burglars will not even attempt to enter, and if they are bold enough to try to crack it then they can reasonably expect the police to arrive before they can even hope to be successful, unless they've bypassed your alarm system. I am referring to what is known as a burglar-class safe. If you want APS-ASDA insurance to cover you, you're going to have to get an ER, TL-15 safe.

Generally a safe of this caliber is at least 2 feet wide by 2 to 3 feet deep and 4 to 6 feet high. There are much larger sizes as well. The weight must be at least 750 pounds to receive the UL rating of ER, TL-15. Further information and literature on safes is available from the APS Insurance Plan Manager, PO Box 1200 Westminster, MD 21158 (phone 410-876-8833, FAX 410-876-9233).

Before we discuss the next area, I would like to say three words concerning renting store or office space — *one-year lease*. Avoid, at all costs, signing anything longer. In fact, attempt to get in for as little as six months as a trial with assurances of one-year leases to follow if the property meets with your approval. Multi-year or perpetual leases must be cast aside as if they carried a fatal disease. You need every advantage possible.

In my opinion, there are three different kinds of shows (or bourses if you will) that are appropriate for you to consider. One is the local weekend bourse, often known by such clever names as "Fourth Sunday" and "Second Saturday." It is held in the same old dimly-lit room on that particular day, month in and month out. There are no exhibits, hence the name "bourse" instead of "show." We also could classify the local stamp club's annual show in this category. It's usually a small affair that features twenty or fewer dealers and a few exhibits by club members. Smaller part-time dealers who do not have much depth of stock have most of the tables. At such events, the more established part-time or full-time dealer has a decided advantage.

Next we have the more regional two-day show, put on by ASDA, a club or clubs, or a private firm. Finally, there are the three- and four-day national shows sponsored or sanctioned by APS or ASDA. They usually are held at major metropolitan hotels. Here we encounter the larger part-time dealers and the full-time professionals who travel the show circuit. More and better exhibits are the rule here, along with state and national society meetings, society booths, sometimes a U.N. or other postal administration representative, and occasionally a U.S.P.S. first-day ceremony. Seminars also are scheduled on many topics by nationally known speakers. You'll typically find 50 to 100 dealers at these nationals.

The biggest of the national shows are the ASDA Mega-Events and the APS STaMpsHOW, which is held in a different location at the end of each August. The larger and better known dealers are here. A room of 125 is common. We'll acknowledge, but rule out for now, the international shows. If you have sufficient capital and stock for them, any advice I could give you would be superfluous.

If you decide to do local bourses, work as many as your time permits. You will want a minimum test of six months to decide whether to continue attending each event. If a new bourse is started, extend the test to at least a year to reach a fair decision. Stay with the ones that are successful for you and drop the rest. It's that simple.

Try to get into a regional or national show if you are fortunate enough to have one nearby. If not, consider traveling to one or two well-known ones. Make sure, however, your inventory is adequate. I'll have plenty to say about that a bit later as I answer the age-old question, "How much stock is enough?" After a few years, you'll probably be ready for the biggest shows. Remember that only members can do the ASDA and APS shows.

Being a show dealer may satisfy the egos of some dealers who feel important sitting behind a table with their name above it. Others enjoy the person-to-person contact. Some love the travel from town to town and socializing in the evenings. Whatever pleases you about being a show dealer, the underlying motivation must be profit. Don't think profit is only measured in dollars and cents, however.

After painstakingly adding up gross receipts, subtracting the cost of the articles sold, and further deducting all associated costs, the neophyte dealer is either chagrined by a minus figure at the end of the tape or ecstatic at a healthy profit. It's nice to return home with more money than you had when the trip began. However, this is not the main reason astute dealers go to shows.

A large mail-order dealer may want to go to several shows each year to meet clients he or she knows only by letter or phone. The dealer also could have been offered a substantial collection to purchase near the same town as the show and could have arranged the purchase to coincide with the show. Another dealer might have one or two pet shows after becoming firmly established as either a retail store, office, or mail-order dealer. He or she still attends those shows every year out of loyalty, habit, devotion, or for some other underlying reason. Still other established dealers attend shows nearly every weekend, some going to as many as 40 or more in a year. Some of them have built up large followings and probably go to buy some good material, rather than to sell enough material to cover expenses.

If you view attending shows as bottom-line events, you'll be disappointed unless being a show dealer is your only business. Sure you'll do well some days. You might even net several hundred dollars for a day's work after expenses. But learn to take the good with the bad. You'll have days when all you'll do is sit on your hands and have a tendency to complain.

What is the main reason a professional dealer takes a booth at a show? Contacts. The toughest part of being a stamp dealer is buying material. Anyone can sell a stamp. It takes a specific skill to replenish stamp stock at the right price.

Shows are sources of collectors looking to sell collections. However, don't expect them to flock in with albums under their arms, anxious to sell to anyone who remotely resembles a stamp dealer. Collectors scrutinize stamp dealers. A collector may spend a day or two sizing up dealers at a show. Who is friendly, knowledgeable, courteous, and honest? Then the dealer gets a call a few days after the show from someone the dealer vaguely remembers meeting. How would the dealer like to purchase a collection of early United States? You bet the dealer would!

Contacts also include the important face-to-face meetings and dealings with your mail-order clients. For a particular customer with big spending habits, you'll probably want to treat the family to a nice dinner.

Then, there's the opportunity to do wholesale business. If you have holes to fill in your stock, what better way than to choose from the variety available to you at a show? Buying is the driving force behind collector attendance at shows, and it's important for dealers, too.

The contacts you make will be important parts of your profit from shows. Ask yourself, "Will I be able to make some important contacts that will pay off somewhere down the road? What value do I place on these potential contacts?" How will that help offset costs of attending the show? Carefully study transportation, lodging, meals, table fees, and other expenses. Think about your profit margin, including contacts. How much stock will you need to sell to cover these expenses? To make a profit?

Next, ask yourself, "What show(s) should I consider doing at first?" In the beginning, work your local weekend bourse for at least six months to truly test the your ability to sell profitably at shows. Next, consider traveling. If there is a three-day show within a day's drive, check at your library or telephone company for a copy of the business directory of that city. If a city of 500,000 people has only two or three dealers listed, it is obviously a philatelic backwater. If you see a dozen or more dealers listed, make your reservations at once.

Unfortunately, there is no formula to help you become or remain a show dealer. You must make the final determination. You must decide if you can justify the expenses. You must evaluate the contacts you have either made or expect to make. There are many factors to weigh very carefully. And, like they say in lottery ads, "You can't win, if you don't play."

There's no doubt about it — the hustle and bustle on a bourse floor full of dealers and collectors is stimulating. However, it's not for everyone. Some dealers are uncomfortable relating with people one on one. Some even dislike people to the extent that they do not want face-to-face or voice contact. Whatever their reasons, they would probably be failures as bourse dealers or selling from a store or office. That brings us to mail order.

There are many reasons to choose a philatelic mail-order career. Maybe you just don't have enough time to do anything else. Your steady job demands most of your attention as you test the field before taking the plunge. Perhaps you've dabbled in stamps for a while, and your inventory isn't really suited for any activity other than mail order.

Whatever the reason, you'll find plenty of company in mail order stamp dealing. Many of today's successful dealers do only mail order.

Most of the others, in fact, began their careers as mail-order practitioners. Actually, most stamp dealers make at least some portion of their sales by mail.

The key question to ask yourself is, "Do I want to do mail order partially, primarily, or solely?" To help you to decide, let's review the other methods of selling:

RETAIL STORE: If you decide on this setting then you will be spending most of your available time serving the needs of your clientele. You will have enough spare time to do a bit of mail order on the side. You may not be able to put out a price list that contains the depth of stock listings that a mail-order specialist would have, nor will your customer list be as large. Finally, retail store prices must be higher than a streamlined mail-order operation because of higher overhead.

You risk pricing yourself out of the market or infuriating your local customers when they inevitably find out you are charging lower mail prices. I would have one set of prices for both the walk-in trade and mail-order accounts. You can use special bonuses and discounts as ways of simultaneously stimulating mail-order sales and discounting from your mail-order price list without seeming unfair to your retail customers.

As success comes, you can expand the mail-order operation if you wish, taking it to the point of hiring specific people to work it. Speaking of success, a few words to the wise: Success comes in time to those who solidly build their reputations and foundations. Success does not present itself for the asking. It is worked for and earned.

OFFICE: Depending on the time you plan to spend on face-to-face relationships with your walk-in customers, mail order can be either a partial or primary venture for a dealer working out of an office. Again, have one set of prices for all customers. An office dealer also is wise to become involved with some shows. Local bourses are excellent vehicles for attracting new customers, and you might consider some regional or national shows as well. You'll have the time for it.

SHOWS: The number of shows that you do will dictate what, if any, involvement you may have with a mail order. (I know some dealers who actually work 50 shows a year.) A few show dealers put out a price list now and then; most do not. I would think a list would increase a show dealer's business substantially, especially a dealer who travels across the entire country. When I worked shows, I also sold by mail, and it was sure nice to have those customers visit you with your price list in hand so that they could pick out their chosen stamps from your stockbooks. And that's the key — there are still many people out there who will not order by mail.

MAIL ORDER: The dealer who initially chooses to enter mail order will eventually face a reverse decision. "Do I stay in mail order exclusively, or do I consider doing some shows, opening a store or office, or some happy combination of the alternatives?" Had these words been written during the boom years of the late 1970s, I would have suggested going for everything. Back then, we had a saying, "If it looks like a stamp, it will sell for more tomorrow than it will bring today." If this had been written during the middle 1980s and early 1990s, I would say, "Cut back on expenses. Times are tough. Stick with mail order, and hope you can make it."

Hindsight is always perfect. The best I can offer without having mystic power is that you must decide on your own course. You will be wise to consider making mail order a significant source of your philatelic revenue. Mail order plays an important part in the lives of so many of today's working families. As more and more people turn to the mails, this market can only prosper.

If you have chosen to do mail order exclusively, you will have certain advantages not available to other dealers. Your main objective each day will be to visit your post office box to collect those lovely orders. The rest of the day is yours. Spend it on your stamp business, though. If you go fishing too often, you'll soon be in another line of work. Fill your orders and answer the important correspondence daily. It is unprofessional to do otherwise and will hurt your career as a stamp dealer.

After your orders are filled, you may want to examine auction lots one particular afternoon. Or you may decide to visit a few of your colleagues in the city to replenish your stock while at the same time you offer some nice stamps to them. Or you may just want to catch up on some philatelic reading or research. It doesn't matter. You are free to set your own schedule. Just be sure you have one. You'll have to budget your time if you want to be successful.

A typical schedule for one day could look like this (it could easily change 180 degrees for the next day):

9 a.m.   — Visit post office for box mail.
9:30   — Open and separate mail.
10:00   — Fill orders and check inventory levels.
Noon   — Lunch and rest break.
1 p.m.   — Answer correspondence.
2:30   — Make bank deposit.

3:00	—	Attend to want-list requests and balance of correspondence from today's important pile or the remainder of yesterday's mail.
4:30	—	Take the mail to the post office.
5:00	—	Dinner and rest break.
6:00	—	Philatelic reading and research.
8:30	—	Prepare schedule for same day of the week next week.

The idea here, as evidenced by the 8:30 p.m. entry, is to always have a week's schedule in front of you. Not counting the breaks, you have a 10-hour day in our example. Don't worry! The days will grow much longer as you grow in stature. Believe me, 18-hour days are more common than you might expect. On the other hand, there is no finer way to make a living. There is no profession that can bring as much pleasure as philately if you are in love with it.

VESTPOCKET DEALING: You'll see them at the bourses. They used to be called satcheleers because of the bags they carried. Sadly, the word is not recognized today in *Webster's Ninth Collegiate Dictionary*. However, at least the word's spirit is with us.

Vestpocket dealers are important. They carry around popular material, some of it on consignment from other dealers, me included. They wholesale it to bourse dealers on weekends and during the week to shopkeepers and office dealers. It's a wonderful way to fill those gaping holes in your stock, and it's tremendously convenient. Who knows? You might even consider doing this yourself. Your profits could be plowed right back into additional stock as you build up your beginning inventory. The best part is that you'll have no significant expenses outside of your car.

If you decide to become a vestpocket dealer, remember one important point. Never, never sell to anyone on the bourse floor who is not a dealer. Don't let anyone convince you to "meet at the coffee shop later." Once word gets out that you sold from under your dealers, you'll get no more business from the dealers who provide your living.

Chapter 4
Advertising

There is one word so powerful it may determine your success or failure. It carries so much weight most dealers treat it as budget Priority No. 1. The ones who don't, overlook it at their peril. The word is *advertising*. It brings you sales and the "R&R" combo of recognition and reputation.

It's not a variable or discretionary expense. It's overhead, just like rent and utilities. I budget 5 percent of my gross sales for advertising. Successful full-time stamp dealers whom I know allocate anywhere from 3 to 6 percent for it. They know they need it to stay in business and to grow. Most small businesses in the U.S. spend less than 3 percent on advertising, and most small businesses fail.

To be successful though, an ad must "pull" enough replies to do the job you want. An ad that offers specific items for sale at fixed prices is often called a "listing." Here you'll see an arrangement of columns consisting of catalog numbers, grade and whether or not the stamp or set is used or unused. The final column shows the price.

The most successful ad brings in enough orders for profits from sales to exceed the cost of the ad. If that's the only measure you use, however, you could be squandering your advertising investment. A $300 ad could bring $200 in profit from sales and several new customers. On the face of it you lost $100. If the sales to the new customers over the coming year bring in $500 profit, though, you're $400 ahead of where you would have been had you not run the ad.

And even an ad that is a failure by all measures is not sufficient grounds for throwing in the towel. There are many reasons ads fail. Among them are poor design and prices that are too high. Often, the design and prices are fine, and it's a matter of a newer dealer needing exposure. When potential customers see your name and ads over and over, they begin to think of you as an established dealer and are willing to try purchasing from you. If they do think of you as established, they then need to see your ad at the time they are ready to buy. A collector who has just lost his or her job may continue to read avidly about stamps without doing any purchasing. Then, when he or she finds another job and is ready to buy from you, your ad must be there or the sale will go to one of your competitors.

Advertising industry studies show that it takes an average of six exposures for a consumer to identify, think about and then act, positively or negatively, towards an ad. This is why you must advertise repetitively. If you question this, think about yourself as a consumer. Do you really think about an advertisement and make a decision the first time you hear it or see it? I don't.

Some collectors may notice your ad the first time and then wait to see if your prices go up or down. Others may see it the first time and comparison shop for several weeks. Most probably will *see* your ad the first time and begin to *look* at it about the sixth time.

Perseverance is the watchword then for your first ad. Have five more ready and place them in succeeding issues or every other week. If you stretch them across 12 weeks it may actually seem longer than that to the collector reading your ads. That can help you achieve the all-important recognition you need.

Another kind of ad might be called a "hook" ad. It's designed with one function in mind – to add collectors to the dealer's mailing list. The "hook," or offer, is often a free price list or the opportunity to be placed in your mailing list, perhaps a special offers or mail-bid list.

Whenever I run this kind of ad, I target my names, or replies, to cost no more than 50 cents each. If my classified ad costs $3 an issue, I expect at least six responses a week. If my display ad costs me $30, I expect at least 60 responses. Ads of this nature are usually kept small because of cost. The facts of business are such that a full-page ad costing $1,000 or more is simply not going to draw 2,000 replies. As a matter of fact, 200 would be good.

An ad that features both a product or products and a hook offers the best of both worlds. Here's an example of a nifty little 4-inch ad that could do very well:

BABY ZEPP ON SALE
(ILLUSTRATION)
WOULDN'T IT LOOK GREAT IN YOUR
COLLECTION? YOU BET IT WOULD!
REGULAR PRICE $85
SUPER SALE PRICE $75
F-VF NH

You've just made an outstanding buy on a quantity of Baby Zepps (Scott C18). To do so, however, you had to take in 40. Your sales history dictates keeping eight on hand. Now you've got a decision to make:

• You could wholesale the surplus inventory to another dealer and make a few dollars per stamp profit.

• You could keep them in stock and await their eventual sale, if your checkbook permits.

• You could do the sensible thing.

Create an attractive ad and offer the stamp at a legitimate savings from your regular price. Don't advertise an $85 regular price if your price list or previous ad never had the stamp listed at that price. Be honest with your customers. They'll reward you for it.

In our example, the product is your Baby Zepp at a special price. Your hook is the free price list. Mail will come from both directions. If you sell enough Baby Zepps to profit from the ad, you'll be able to add valuable names free to your mailing list.

Another kind of ad you'll see frequently is called institutional. It promotes a company's name and services. Large auction companies frequently use institutional ads to call attention to spectacular prices realized. The idea is to catch the attention of potential consignors. Stamp companies that continually advertise to buy collections and accumulations often use institutional advertising. They want their names to be remembered by collectors when the time comes to sell. Institutional ads project your company's image and enhance its name without offering products for sale.

What kind of ad is best for you?

LISTING: The fledgling dealer needs depth of stock and perseverance to use listing ads. It takes several issues to achieve recognition. Once you get rolling, these are the most profitable ads.

HOOK: Strongly recommended for the newcomer who wants to build a mailing list. A 25- to 35-word classified ad run every week is the best bet here. Later in this chapter I'll give you specifics on classifieds.

PRODUCT & HOOK: An enterprising newcomer or established dealer can look for opportunities to buy popular items in quantity at a good price. He or she then can feature them in 2- to 4-inch classified display ads that also offer collectors the opportunity to get on his or her mailing list.

INSTITUTIONAL: Reserved for the larger, well-established dealer who wants to promote the firm's achievements or reputation. This is the other half of the "R&R" combo that we mentioned earlier. There is nothing that says that a new dealer can't use institutional advertising. If, for example, you are starting out with a list of early U.S. used classics in choice condition, you could put in a small classified display ad every week in addition to your other ads.

If you're a new dealer, you really can't budget a portion of sales toward advertising because there is no track record. What you must do is make a projection on expected revenue. Let's say you are going to invest $10,000 in a beginning inventory. A reasonable expectation would be to "turn over" your inventory four times a year. This means you are expecting to do $40,000 in sales volume a year.

Five percent of your expected sales yields an advertising budget of $2,000. With this in mind, you certainly can't run full-page ads. If you run listing ads, you may want to go 8 to 10 inches an ad for four or five insertions. A steadily running classified ad or two is an excellent idea.

While most dealers limit their ads to the philatelic press, some also use mass-circulation publications. *Popular Mechanics* magazine is one example. Only a small percentage of its vast readership actually collects stamps to any degree. The people who do seem to be mostly general collectors of low-priced foreign sets, and they are prime candidates for approval dealers. In a mass-circulation publication, you pay the going rate to reach every reader. However, your cost per collector or serious stamp prospect reached is much higher. This is true of every publication targeted to a wide audience.

The advantage of advertising in the philatelic press is that your advertising dollars are spent to reach stamp collectors only. Your cost per potential client is reduced greatly.

No matter what type of ad you run and where you run it, AIDA is the key to results for you. That acronym means:

A (for ATTENTION) All successful ads capture the attention of readers. Ads that aren't read don't produce results. Look at the Baby Zepp ad again. The attention getters are the headline, "BABY ZEPPS ON SALE," and the illustration. A picture of a beautiful stamp is a powerful reader stopper.

I (for INTEREST) You must interest prospects in your offer, and you have a limited space to cast your bait. In our sample ad the picture not only attracts attention, it adds interest. Along with the idea of a money-saving sale, it is half of a double-play combination for interest and attention at the same time. First, we got the reader's attention, and now we have her interested in what we have to offer.

D (for DESIRE) Although you're close to getting the order, you have more work to do. Your prospect is still dangling. She's not totally convinced. You must spark her desire. Our ad does this admirably well by saying, "WOULDN'T IT LOOK GREAT IN YOUR COLLECTION? YOU BET IT WOULD!" At this point, the collector hopefully will begin to envision the pleasure of adding that lovely stamp to her album. The clincher is your "SUPER SALE PRICE," which clearly shows a sizable savings. Even if the collector already has the stamp, you can whet her appetite to request your price list. These are exactly the kinds of collectors you want on your mailing list. The ones who spend that kind of money on stamps will be going after more stamps of similar or higher-price.

A (for ACTION) Now, we've done everything possible to land the order, short of actually asking for it. It's time to induce action from the collector. Our ad says "LIMITED TO STOCK ON HAND. ORDER TODAY." In other words, buy it right away so you will be sure of getting it. We go even further by including Visa and MasterCard logos to make it easy to buy on impulse and pay later.

When you add everything together, it now is an ad that does everything we can do to maximize sales. Advertising professionals charge hefty fees to write ads using the AIDA approach. You now possess the secret to use whenever you want to create your own highly successful ads.

Classified ads in philatelic publications offer low-cost, effective ways of attracting new customers. Often the proving grounds of newer dealers, the classified section also is the Mecca of established dealers who want to keep their names in front of the public and to gain customers to replace those lost through attrition.

To make your mark in classified word ads though, your ad has to stand out from others and it must be read. Publications like *Stamp Collector* newspaper offer stars (★), bullets (•) and centered headlines to capture the reader's attention. I strongly suggest their use as sure-fire eye-stoppers. Before you can keep the reader's attention, you need to grab it. And you are not only competing with hundreds of other ads in the same paper, but you are also doing battle with other print and electronic media and every distraction that is a normal part of daily life.

How do you accomplish your goal? By applying that word *AIDA* again. The headline, star or bullet will catch the attention of the reader. Interest will be generated by the opening offer. Spark desire with your product or service and the ways it benefits the reader. Then, prompt action by telling the customer to do it today, or do it now or that the offer expires in 10 days. Let's take a look now at a classified ad that has the four necessary components of AIDA.

FREE

$1.00 Discount Coupon and our new price list featuring accurately graded mint and used U.S. stamps at competitive prices. Member ASDA. VISA - MasterCard. Write today. Eagle Stamps (since 1968), Box 221, Dept. SC, Anytown, ST 00000.

Your attention was focused on the bold headline **FREE**. You became interested in the $1 discount coupon and new price list. Desire was aroused by a dealer who could supply you with accurately graded stamps at competitive prices. The assurance that the dealer was an ASDA member allowed your desire to quiet your caution. Action was prompted by the words *write today.*

But wait a moment. The collector might be thinking, "I can't buy the stamps I want for a month or two. I've got to pay those unexpected bills first. Oh well, I guess all the better items will be grabbed by someone else. Wait a minute! Eagle Stamps accepts charge cards. I can get the stamps I want now! Where's my pen?" This is the advantage, my friends, of accepting charge cards. You get additional sales and inquiries that help your advertising investment pay off to the maximum.

This ad has all the earmarks of success. By actual word count we have the headline, (which normally counts as five words when it's in larger centered type) and 35 words in the body for a total of a 40-word ad. Your natural tendency might be to trim the ad to 25 words to pay as little as possible for it. Such savings are illusions. If you cut 15 words from this ad, you will save yourself the bother of filling orders you would have gotten with a longer ad that took the space necessary to sell your product or services as well as possible. In general, you make your money in stamps by buying smart – not by practicing false advertising economy. Avoid being like the dealer who was proud that he did not need to advertise to reach collectors. The first ad he placed was for his going-out-of-business sale.

Now let's analyze our sample ad a bit further. The discount coupon is a difficult-to-resist get-acquainted offer. Everyone likes to receive a gift, and I've had good success offering $1 off an initial $10 offer. Also, remember to put an expiration date on the coupon as an incentive for the collector to value the coupon more highly and to respond more quickly. Any response that is put off becomes a response you never may get.

A new price list is mentioned. New is one of the so-called "key" words that inspires a positive reaction. Key words are used by successful advertisers to perform the tasks required by our good friend AIDA. Our headline, **FREE,** is one of the best key words. Others in our ad include *discount, featuring, accurately, competitive* and *today.* Key phrases in the ad are *member ASDA*, which proclaims your proud affiliation with that organization. *VISA-MasterCard* indicates that you care enough about customer convenience to accept payment by charge cards, even though it costs you money to do so. *Since 1968* displays the undeniable fact that you are long-established. It subliminally implies that if you have been in business this long, you must be reliable and must be taking care of customers.

Here are a few examples of dynamite words that were found in the classified ads of other dealers in four pages of one issue of *The Stamp Wholesaler.* Many of these words appeared in several different ads:

Free, Reduced, Sale, Special, Limited, Today, Now, Bonus, Service, Best, Quality, New, Discount, Featuring, Gorgeous, Satisfied, Complete, Accurate, Excellent, Attention, Competitive, Guaranteed, Bargain, Immediate, Fast, Prompt, Licensed, Sample, Write, Extensive, Save, Great, Exceptional, Send, Super, Better, Reliable, Honest, Welcomed, Perfect.

The list is far from complete. You can find and use other key words in your ads. What are the words that grab or inspire you to thought or to action?

Besides dynamite words, there is another key to use if you are running the same ad in several publications at the same time. It is the address key, or tracer. Our sample ad contained the address *Dept. SC.*

Envelopes addressed to you in this manner will tell you that the ad was read in *Stamp Collector*. You could use *Dept. TT* for your ad in *Topical Time* magazine, etc.

However, some collectors are wise to the use of such designations and will leave them off when writing to you.

Keying your ads is important because even though you have a super ad, one that you can't find fault with, it may pull much better in one publication than another. Perhaps a different mix of collectors reads one publication than another. Perhaps your ad ran in a special issue in this publication or that one, or one that had a larger press run for distribution as sample copies. By keeping a running scorecard, you'll know where your best results are coming from. You'll also be able to tell when a single ad excels or bombs or when the readers of a certain publication aren't responding to your ads.

When a publication isn't working for you, it's time to redo the ad in that publication or to invest your ad money elsewhere. You can imagine that an ad geared to the members of the American First Day Cover Society might not work as well in the American Topical Association magazine without being reworded to move the emphasis from FDCs to topical stamps.

For the publication that isn't pulling, you also might consider redesigning your ad or trying a different classification. Picking the best classification can be tricky at times. My price list ads appear under the "Unused U.S. For Sale" heading. I chose it because most of my stock is unused and because I tried other sections that just didn't yield the same results. Previously I tried U.S. Miscellaneous, Price Lists and Announcements categories.

Your placement helps to pre-qualify potential clients. After all, if they're reading the Unused U.S. section, they must have a genuine interest in those stamps. If I decide to expand my stock to include a greater portion of used stamps I'll place another ad in the Used U.S. For Sale classification.

Another tip: I found out the expensive way that most responses to my ads in the Announcements and Price Lists classifications brought out the treasure hunters, or cherry pickers. They're the collectors who send for all the free offers without intending to become customers. Often, they only want updated information on the value of their holdings. Most publications have them, and there seems to be a higher percentage in some publications than others. However, collectors who pick cherries from one ad may be buyers from an ad next to it. Testing for yourself is the only way to find out where the collectors are who like your kind of stock and service.

Before testing the waters study the classified sections carefully. Clip ads that catch your attention. Analyze them. Put yourself in the collector's position. (A) What caught your eye? (I) What made you interested? (D) What made you want the offer? (A) What prompted you to respond?

When you're ready to write your ad have some key words in mind. Be clear and concise. The first copy might not be quite right. Be prepared to rewrite and then rewrite again.

Are you going to offer a premium? Our sample ad offered a $1 discount coupon that really was a kind of premium. If you offer a coupon, rubber stamp an expiration date that will be 30 days from the date you mail it. That affords ample time for a collector to order and still puts him or her under deadline pressure.

Another tip: If a customer or potential customer returns a coupon after the deadline date, honor it anyway if you still have the stock or ability to do so. Forget trying to make customers live by your rules. You are dealing with collectors who are used to having their local stores honor even outlandish requests in the name of good customer service. They like being pampered and catered to, and they will richly reward stamp dealers who treat them the way the dealers would like to be treated in reverse. They'll also be more likely to treat you respectfully. You probably will be surprised at the collectors who you go out of your way for on something minor and who turn into profitable customers you never would have developed had you been hard nosed. When you are a stamp dealer, it costs you money to be picky, surly or to lash out at others.

Instead of discount coupons, some dealers offer a popular stamp or set at a discount price to get names for their list. An example is an offer of a set of unhinged, fine to very-fine 1934 National Parks priced $2 below the prevailing market. Let's say you bought 100 or more sets quite cheaply and you can still make a profit by offering them below market. The upside is you could attract some buyers who become good customers. The downside is that you'll probably attract a lot of bargain hunters.

They'll have no loyalty to you and no appreciation for your extra professionalism and service. They'll go anywhere to save a few cents. You can do without them. If you accept their invitation to "dance," you'll receive innumerable requests to "do a bit better in price" or questions like, "So and so has the same set $5 cheaper; why are your prices so high?" I recommend writing ads that discourage them. I also suggest you simply fill an order and drop them from your list when you spot one. If correspondence is necessary, write once and say courteously something to the effect that you regret you are not able to supply their needs and recommend that they try another dealer who may better be able to serve them. Spend your time with loyal customers.

And modify your ads to minimize cherry picking. Your advertising goal is to convey an image of professionalism. You want to be regarded as an honest dealer who grades properly and prices fairly. Your reputation comes first. By writing your ads in the right tone, you will tell your customers what kind of business you operate and what kind of customers you want to serve. They not only will recognize you as their kind of dealer, they'll reward you the best way they can – by ordering.

Display advertising serves the same purpose as classified. It's a way to offer your goods and services to the public and to polish the image of your company. With classified, one of the advantages is having your ads appear with others in a special section at the back of the publication that is conveniently categorized and heavily shopped by readers in a buying mood. That's why it can be to your advantage to run small display ads in classified. The organization of the section helps your ad be found and compete with larger ads scattered throughout the publication.

With display, your ad may appear anywhere in the front articles section of the publication and has the advantage of being adjacent to news and features. Advertising studies through the years have indicated that being next to articles increases readership of ads. Philatelic newspapers will accept large, and even full-page, display ads in their classified sections. That means in a paper like *Stamp Collector* that has illustrated classified, virtually the same large ad could run anywhere in the paper. Except for supplies and accessories, however, most stamp dealers prefer to run their large display ads in the front sections. Whether rightly or wrongly, they consider the articles sections to be the prestigious places.

To state the obvious, large display ads create greater visibility and have space to offer more of your goods and services or to create an upscale image of your business through the artistic use of layout, illustration and white space. How much greater attention large ads draw depends on their size and some other variables.

White space is one important ingredient of a successful display ad. That's right! Paying for blank space is one of the smartest things you can do. *The Wall Street Journal* periodically has ads with only a few words on an entire page. Almost *every* reader reads them.

When you jam too much in your ad to get every last stamp listed, you invariably create an ad that looks discouraging to readers. The result? Your ad is skipped, and your competitor's ad that looks inviting because of artful use of white space gets the business. In short, an inviting ad will be read; and that's half the battle.

Next, the judicious use of illustrations does more than dress up an ad. Photos show collectors how you grade and increase their desire for your stamps. Readers can see exactly what you mean when you say "very fine" or "lightly canceled." A picture really is worth 1,000 words.

Use color whenever you can, also. An ad with a color like red, blue or yellow used for some of the boxes, some of the headlines or as a background block behind some areas costs more. However, tests indicate that readership and responses can increase by 50 percent or more over the same ad with black ink only. The increased response can more than repay the modest additional amounts philatelic newspapers charge for one additional color of their choice.

One of the best ways to create successful display ads is to build an advertising reference library that can become as valuable as your philatelic reference collection. Clip display ads that catch your eye. What did it? The headline? The illustration? The uncluttered appearance that includes generous space between each line? The white space surrounding the blocks of type and illustrations? The color?

Notice ads that are poor, too. Does the headline mislead readers? Does an illustration seem out of keeping with the ad? Is there a lot of cutesy, needless chatter? Refrain from saying things like "These babies are sure to double in value real soon," "Boy it is sure hot down here; the heat must have got me good to price these stamps so cheeeeap." A few dealers are skillful at using such images to move certain kinds of stamps. Unless you're very sure of what you're doing, however, you'll do a lot better to convey an image of knowledgeable professionalism

Use your ad reference library to see how many items you can fit effectively into a 4-inch, 8-inch or whatever-size ad you're preparing. You'll be able to judge the space you'll need for the headline, terms, listing and address. Whatever you come up with, add an inch for good measure to ensure ample white space and proper size type. Then send the ad in.

Be sure to make liberal use of the help available from advertising representatives at the stamp publications. The people at the publications are there to help you. Happy advertisers are steady advertisers. Often a telephone call on the publications' toll-free numbers will produce the aid you need from professionally trained ad reps.

More and more stamp dealers also are finding it increases their business to use toll-free telephone numbers. In the beginning, however, you'll probably want to stick with your regular business number. Be sure to include it in your ads. You could be pleasantly surprised at the number of calls you get as you become established.

Offering the use of VISA and MasterCard can make it easy for collectors to order by phone. And advertising your membership in a respected organization can increase reader confidence in responding to your ad. Instead of saying "Member ASDA" or "Member APS," have the newspaper use the appropriate logos. Those ASDA triangles and APS monograms are real eye-catchers in advertisements. The VISA and MasterCard signs can help your ad, too.

Establish an order deadline to protect yourself from latecomers who seem to respond only when the value of a stamp goes up. Phrases such as "Prices good for 30 days after date of publication" or "Prices good until sold out" are effective disclaimers. They also are motivators for readers to order because they imply limited quantities are on hand and immediate action is necessary.

Testimonials can be useful, too. If, for example, one of your satisfied customers says in a letter, "I have never experienced such prompt, courteous service. Nor have I encountered such accurate grading or fair pricing in my 25 years of collecting," run to your computer and get off an immediate thank-you letter asking for permission to use the letter as a testimonial in your ads. To increase the likelihood of receiving permission, you even can offer a gift of stamps or something else as a way of saying thank you for using the letter.

Tell your client that you simply will use his or her name and state, or – if he or she specifically requests it – you'll use initials only with the city and state. Enclose two copies of your letter and ask your client to sign and date one and return it in the stamped addressed envelope you've also enclosed. That way, you write the agreement as you want it, and you make it exceptionally easy for your client to respond favorably. No one ever has ever turned down my request to use a testimonial. As a matter of fact, the above testimonial is one I actually received.

Two tips on testimonials: Keep the original correspondence in your legal files in case you are ever asked to produce it, and always label testimonials in your ads as unsolicited. Testimonials can do more to enhance your image than you possibly can imagine. Run them as frequently as you can. Two or three per ad will have double or triple the effect.

It's so easy to fall in love with your own ads that some newer dealers think a Postal Service truck will pull up at curbside to unload sacks upon sacks of lovely orders each day. When the inevitable happens (your ad doesn't pull as well as expected), the tendency is to start pointing fingers at someone or something else. Suddenly, the collector becomes ignorant of superior values. You were going to treat the customer like royalty by sending out accurately graded stamps at money-saving prices. Why are collectors ignoring you and your ads? Why are they wasting money away elsewhere when you know that you can easily beat all of your competition on service and quality? Reread this chapter, and learn the meaning of perseverance and of trial and error.

Or maybe your ad looks like every other dealer's. If you can't come up with original layouts, or if the advertising people at the publications can't deliver exactly what you want, perhaps it's time to consult an agency or commercial artist. Be prepared to pay professional fees that may seem as large to you as your appraisal fees seem to some unknowledgeable collectors.

Perhaps you suspect you advertised at the wrong time of year. Hogwash. Advertising is right, and necessary, 52 weeks all year. True, summer might not be the best time to feature "big ticket" items as collectors' thoughts turn to nice vacation spots, but it is a great time for you to buy from collectors. Vacations cost money. What better way to help collectors finance trips than by purchasing some of their lovely stamps? As I'll continue to repeat, you make your money in this business by buying smart.

Another lame excuse for poor ad results is, "The magazine really killed me. My ad was surrounded by six others that had my prices beat on just about everything." I call that suicide, not murder. Unless you have a strong reputation for delivering a superior product with lightning personal service and your grading is known to be ultra-conservative compared with a competitor who grossly overgrades, you have nobody but yourself to blame. When comparing apples with apples, your customer inevitably will end up in the orchard that offers the best quality at a fair price.

So, rather than fall into the victim trap, I recommend you take strong measures to create strong ads that create the kind of commercial future you want. Aim for having not only the best ad on the page but the best ad in the publication. Be aware of your competition and compete vigorously. Advertise regularly. And above all, be patient.

Chapter 5
Inventory

New dealers discover quickly that buying stamps is much tougher than selling them. Although there are many sources of supply, it's hard going for newcomers until they become "known" in the trade. Promoting yourself with small display ads that are published regularly in the philatelic press is the fastest path to recognition. It's an effective way to advise potential business connections, both dealer and collector, that you are an active buyer and seller in your specialty.

You also can increase recognition of your business by interspersing your ads with news releases that gain you valuable notice you cannot buy. Address your releases to the editor, using his or her name from a recent issue of the publication. Allow four to six weeks from the time you mail until you see your article in print. For example, if you want to promote your latest mail-bid catalog, which has a closing date of Oct. 1, you will want to mail the news release by July 24 at the latest.

This is why:
- One week in the mail to the paper.
- Four weeks minimum for editing and publication.
- Four weeks for the collector to request your catalog, receive it by first-class mail and then bid before the sale closes.

Too often, I've seen news releases in the stamp papers trumpeting some great upcoming event, only to see that the "action" date has either already passed or it will in a couple of days. And many more must have been thrown away by on-the-ball editors who realized they would be too late to help readers if printed when received. Plan ahead!

Realize also that news releases amount to free ads for you. However, editors publish them because they have information that interests readers. The business of publications is to sell papers to readers and to sell ads to dealers. Unless your release has information that really is news, an editor is giving away valuable ad space without getting paid if he or she uses your release. It would be like you being in business to sell stamps and then giving them away instead.

If you're also an advertiser, an editor might give you the benefit of the doubt. Don't count on it, though. Like most stamp dealers, most editors are people of integrity who make every attempt to be fair to all news sources, whether they are advertisers or not. If you suggest they use your news release because you are an advertiser, they may do the opposite. When you make the news release a matter of principle for them, they'll often opt for principle, even if it costs their publication your advertising business.

Since your objective is to get as much free advertising as possible to supplement your paid ads, include two points in the cover letter that accompanies your news release. Tell the editor why your news will interest readers. If you already advertise with the publication, also say something like, "Your readers have been interested in our ads, and we hope this additional information will be useful to them." If you plan to advertise, say something like, "We are hoping to test your advertising soon and would like to present this news to your readers in the meantime."

Then live up to your promise. Editors are intelligent, and they realize that the first time a dealer fools them the dealer usually is just practicing.

A sample news release might read like this:

For Immediate Release	For Further Information
	Peter Mosiondz Jr.
	P.O. Box 1483
	Bellmawr, NJ 08099-5483
	609-627-6865

Peter Mosiondz Jr., is pleased to announce the publication of his new stamp dealer newsletter, "The Intelligent Stamp Dealer™." It is filled with ready-to-use information and helpful hints from which both new dealers and veterans can profit.

A special introductory offer is being made available to all *Stamp Wholesaler* readers who respond by Dec. 31, 1995. One full year, regularly priced at $75, can be purchased for $60 – a 20 percent discount.

The premiere issue is scheduled for release early in 1996. Readers interested in becoming charter subscribers can contact Mosiondz at P.O. Box 1483, Bellmawr, NJ 08099-5483.

A couple of tips. Be sure to specify at the top of the page "For Release on xxxx" or "For Immediate Release." If there is a date involved in the news, the editor must know when to insert it. Be sure to double space on clean, plain 8½x11-inch white paper. Decisions on whether your press release will be published and how it will be edited depend on how important (newsworthy in the editor's opinion) and complete the information is that you provide. The easier you make it for the busy editor to drop it in the way you wrote it, the higher likelihood that it will be used. Read some trade news items in the publication you are aiming at and write your release the same way.

To most quickly build your image and name recognition, and therefore sales and profits, you need both legitimate news releases and paid ads. It's the same principle as a collector needing both a stockbook and an album. They're both useful, and they do different jobs.

As you become known, increasing buying opportunities will come your way, and you'll focus on three primary sources of supply: auctions, purchases directly from collectors, and purchases from wholesalers. Let's examine each, beginning with the sources of supply that require a cash outlay or approved credit terms.

There is not one intelligent stamp dealer who does not use auctions as an ideal source for new and fresh material. Intelligent dealers also buy smart or they do not buy at all. There's a big difference between buying and buying smart. Buying smart does not mean purchasing one of several identical lots at a few dollars less than anyone else spent for the same thing. To buy smart, you must know your stock needs, and you must be acutely aware of your current and projected financial situation. Your payables and receivables must be anticipated for at least 90 days.

Have your accountant draw up a spreadsheet. You will want to see your past performance, current state of affairs and anticipation of future events. This is not to say that every time you want to spend a few hundred dollars you should go to the needless expense of charting your course. You certainly will want to know in advance just how much you can afford to spend at a sale before you make major acquisitions, however.

Identify your auction buying opportunities. Is there another sale coming in a few weeks with similar or better material available? You may want to make some low bids at the first sale. If you get the lots, fine. If not, there's the next sale. Did you recently purchase a sizable collection? Be careful. You don't want to spread yourself too thin.

A signed bid sheet is a legal contract. You are bound to honor your bids. Before bidding, make doubly sure you have the funds to pay for all of the lots you win. Do not fall into the trap of saying, "I don't have to worry about getting all of the lots on which I bid. I'll be lucky to get half of them." If you send in $1,000 worth of bids, make sure you have $1,000 in reserve.

Before circling the lots of interest in the auction catalog, you had better go through your stock books to see exactly what you need. In my office, "going through the books" means looking at a computer printout by Scott catalog number that shows a complete sales history on each U.S. stamp I sell for $5 or more. I see at a glance every grade, used or unused, when bought and at what cost, date sold and at what price. I see what I need, quantities I need and how much I can afford to pay.

From this valuable data, I compile my shopping list of all items that are needed for the upcoming three-month inventory cycle. (I find it extremely profitable not to tie up money for any longer.) I then make up my secondary list. These are the stamps that I'll buy only if they are at least 20 percent less than my usual buy price. Perhaps the best advice I can give you concerning auctions is to *keep your head.* Discipline and planning will serve you well.

After reviewing your stock and analyzing your financial situation, you are ready to attack the auction catalog. I start by highlighting lots. I use pink for lots of primary interest and yellow for secondary lots. And very importantly, either I or my auction agent examine all lots on which I want to bid. Each agent has an agenda of sales to attend. Sometimes it can get quite hairy if Harmer's and Robert A. Siegel are each holding a sale on the same day.

What invariably happens is that two friendly agents get together and represent each other and all clients involved at each sale. I said friendly because it is best to realize now that in this business there are no enemies. You are not doing battle with tough competitors. In this business we are all colleagues. It is this that separates the stamp business from most other trades.

The standard fee an agent charges is 5 percent of the invoice price. For this reasonable amount, you can count on a professional, unbiased examination and opinion of the stamp or collection in question. As far as my agent is concerned, there is no fee if there are no lots won.

If there is a variance in the grading, your agent will advise. Your agent will become sharp as he or she works for you. Your every fetish will become known. If the item is not up to your standards, expect to be told. Once your agent gets to know your stocking requirements, you'll be informed of special opportunities that you might have been unaware of by your not being on a certain auction company's mailing list. Beyond question, an auction agent is worth every cent you pay, and more.

After getting the opinion of your agent or examining the lots yourself, enter your maximum bid next to each lot number in your catalog. Take the buyer's premium, which usually is 10 percent, into consideration. For example, if I want to go no higher than $80 on a given lot and the auctioneer has $5 bidding intervals on lots that are hammered down between $50 and $100, I bid $70 and note this number next to the lot number. If I get it, the lot will cost me $70 plus a $7 commission. If I had gone to a $75 bid, the lot would have cost me $82.50, which would have been above my $80 limit. I'm firm on this rule.

In my novice years, I calculated the cost of postage and factored that into the price that each lot, or stamp, cost me. I drove myself crazy with all the time and trouble. Now, I itemize postage and insurance costs on my records simply as postage expenses. I enter agent commissions as professional fees expenses and assign the remaining amount to inventory costs.

For sales I attend in person, I keep running track of what I spend and constantly compare it with my overall budget for the sale. Once I reach my predetermined total, I stop. The only exception I make is when one of my "pink" wanted items can be had for at least 20 percent less than the price I was willing to pay.

Here are some other tips: (1) Read and understand the conditions of sale. (2) Ask the auctioneer, no later than the day before the sale for the opening bid on any lot that is of interest. (3) Ask the auctioneer, no later than the day before the sale for an estimate on any lot that you are uncertain of the value for. (4) Avoid the euphoria of the auction process. The fever spreads quickly and will cost you money. (5) If bidding by phone, ask for the name of the bid clerk that is assisting you and have your bids read back. (6) Confirm all phone bids in writing. (7) Wait until at least the second business day after the sale to call for prices realized on your lots. (8) Pay all auction bills when they are due.

Auctions can be an excellent source of supply if you play by the rules – theirs and yours.

To do much significant buying, you need a walk-in location, as we discussed in Chapter 3. Once you have your store or office, buying starts with agreeing on price. I have found every seller knows how much he or she wants to receive. Don't do it when a seller says, "Give me your top price." Ask the seller to name the price. The object is to find out what the seller considers fair and to pay it if it's fair to you, too, and you want the collection.

If your party refuses to put a price on it and you really want it, go through it and give the only offer you will make. What probably will happen is that a crestfallen look will appear on the seller's face. He or she may even say you are a thief and that the collection is worth much more. All of this from the same person who earlier said, "Give me your top price." Unless you really want the collection, avoid this process by politely saying, when the seller won't name a price, that the collection doesn't fit your needs and that you're not interested in buying it.

If you are unable to consummate a deal for the whole, any offer you make for a single item can come under the heading of an appraisal. You may be asked to make individual offers for several sets or singles. We'll get into appraisals in the next chapter. For now, just remember that free appraisals are taboo.

Burn into your mind the important rules for dealing with sellers: (1) Always be cordial – ABC, as I keep reminding myself. (2) Have the seller set the price. (3) If you must set the price because you want the collection that much, set one fair price and stick to it. (4) Avoid giving free appraisals.

If you are unable to buy a collection, perhaps you can land it on consignment. The owner (seller) of the stamps must set the price on each portion that will be offered for sale individually, and an agreement (contract) must be signed. These are some of the highlights of an effective consignment contract:

Briefly, it should state "that the owner of the collection fully empowers you to act on his or her behalf for the sale of all or part of the collection, which is described as follows." A list of the selling prices for all or part of the collection should be attached for reference, showing Scott catalog numbers and condition/grade. If there is to be no list of selling prices, the seller stipulates that you are responsible for setting all prices in the seller's best interest and that there can be no future dispute or recourse to your decisions.

Clearly state your commission. Standard rates are 20 percent for minor consignments of $10,000 or less and proportionately less above that amount. Be sure to specify a return date for the unsold remainder. When it is returned, obtain a release from your consignor that stipulates that the transaction has been carried out to his/her complete satisfaction and that full payment has been duly received for all items sold. You can either pay the seller at the period's end, or as I prefer to do, reconcile the account on a monthly basis. I use the 10th of the month to mail my checks for the preceding month of sales activity.

I am not an attorney, and it is important to have your lawyer approve or draw up whatever forms you will use so you will be sure you are protected in your own locale. You can minimize legal costs by compiling the best agreement and release possible from office-supply-store forms and other dealers' forms (if you're lucky enough to have a dealer friend who will share them) and then asking your attorney to modify them as necessary.

A private treaty is basically a consignment property that is intended to be sold as a single unit for some particular reason. You can lower your commission to anywhere between 5 and 10 percent, depending on the collection's net worth. Most private treaty collections are in the "four-figure" price range and require little or no work by you in addition to advertising and listing the property for sale. Your contract with the owner includes everything the consignment contract calls for, except for selling portions of the property.

I once had a chance to purchase a specialized AMG (Allied Military Government) collection. Neither I nor the owner had any idea of the overall worth. There were just too many seldom-seen items, including covers with postmarks that were unfamiliar to me. There was one thing upon which we agreed. The owner certainly was entitled to a nice price. How to obtain it was the question.

I could have recommended public auction or even direct sale to a specialist dealer. I didn't because I remembered a local collector who was fascinated by AMG's and who had asked me to inform him of anything that looked good. I called him and gave a price. "I'll be right down," he replied. Everyone was happy and it had to be one of the shortest times for a private-treaty sale ever. Although I earned only a modest commission, I wish that I could make that sum on an hourly basis!

It was 1983, my second year in my store. The sale amount was $750 and I earned 10% ($75). The seller later told me that would have accepted $100.

The benefits, then, of handling consignment and private treaty properties are new sources of supply and customers and revenue you would have lost otherwise.

There are not that many real *wholesalers* around any more who sell in quantity at less-than-retail prices. Find those you can and try a few with test orders. Evaluate grading, overall quality and pricing. It's a good sign if you must establish dealer status before obtaining a wholesaler's list. Companies that only sell to bonafide dealers really are wholesalers. There also are some wholesale mail-bid sales that will give you the opportunity to purchase popular sets and singles at true wholesale prices. You may even get some nice material for less than published "buy" prices.

The advantage to having a good wholesale source is that you will frequently be given first crack at large lots in your specialty. One of the best places to locate sources is *The Stamp Wholesaler,* 700 East State Street, Iola, WI 54990-0001. You even can phone 1-800-258-0929 and charge a subscription, which could be a tax-deductible cost of doing business, to your VISA or MasterCard. This excellent every-other-week newspaper also is filled with dealer news and tips that are worth many times the modest subscription cost.

Determining the right amount of stock for your business is the difficult question to answer. Any answer depends largely on the kind of dealer you are and your specialty. Because I handle only U.S., I can only address this area with any accuracy. From 1940 on, I don't stock any singles. I'm pleased to do business, though, on the handful of better post-1930s stamps. I'll gladly sell $5 Hamiltons, knowing that I can always pick one up through a wholesaler or at auction.

It's foolish to fill orders for single stamps on which your profit margin is just a few cents each. Let that go until your company is large enough to have one or two part-time employees who can fill those orders for you at a lower cost than your time when you are running the entire business. For now, sell commemorative year sets. Pack them in No. 4½ glassines to allow suitable room for the se-tenant blocks. Assemble them up in your spare time, and perhaps even have your children help. Also sell the U.S. air mails from C32 onward as a set. They will be among your best prepackaged-set sellers.

Keep at least 10 sets each in stock of the commemorative year sets and at least five of the air mails. Here's a tip on marketing the year sets. Add up the individual prices of each year. Take at least 10 percent off and offer the entire run as a special offer for an "instant collection builder."

You may decide to offer definitive sets once you've tasted the success of the commemoratives. For the Liberty set, it can be offered as a short set to the $1 and as a complete set. Ten short and three complete sets will be enough to meet ordinary demands and allow time for replacements to arrive. For the Prominent Americans and Great Americans, three to five should be enough. A package of all the "odds-and-ends" regulars that don't fit into these sets could be offered as well. Keep the stock small; commemoratives sell much more rapidly than definitives.

Package the coil issues by series, both as singles and as pairs. Three of each should be enough until you reach the Transportation set. For the foreseeable future, this set will be virtually flying out of your stock; so go for at least 20 sets of singles and at least that many of pairs.

The series is tremendously popular in PNC (Plate Number Coil) strips of three or five. Some plate numbers sell for hundreds of dollars a strip. Even common numbers can sell for unbelievable premiums over face value. Caution is the watchword here. The basic sets of plain pairs and singles will always be popular. Be leery of laying out big bucks for those PNC strips of three and five.

What does the future hold for this fad? Maybe the word *fad* sums it up. Fads come and go. The tiny plate numbers apparently were placed on the stamps by the USPS to create new revenue from collectors. PNC popularity has exceeded everyone's expectations. Eventually, the killing-the-goose-that-laid-the-golden-egg principle will kick in.

I'm afraid of any volatile stamps. Prices can slide as rapidly as they rise. I expect interest in PNC's to drop as prices climb. Prices will reach high enough levels to squeeze many collectors out of the marketplace. At some point, there will be more sellers than buyers. After all, is it really that important to have a couple dozen different tiny plate numbers on the same stamp? The current PNC market is reminiscent of the heyday of collecting plate blocks in matched sets and for every possible number.

As for other U.S. stamps, I keep at least one mint copy of everything that catalogs up to $25 for 90 percent of the issues from 1900 to 1939. I keep from 10 to 20 each of the popular 2c Reds, Washington Bicentennials, National Parks, Farleys, Famous Americans and the like. Another tip: Sell the 2c Reds as a complete unit. When collectors start buying them for their albums, they need all of them, and this makes it more consistent. I also sprinkle some of the postally used stamps of the era in my stockbooks and top them off with a decent showing of approximately half of the higher priced stamps (over $25 catalog value). For the 19th century I have two or three used No. 1's and at least one nice used No. 2. Remember, the deeper your stock, the larger the image of your company. Conversely, the deeper your stock, the greater your investment in inventory. It's a balancing act that changes as your company grows and you can afford to build inventory to attract more customers and as an investment.

Even at the beginning, you'll also need a decent showing of 19th century used stamps to the Columbian Issue to have the image of an established, professional philatelist. For the stamps that catalog up to $100 each, you'll need to be at least 75 percent complete. Focus additional attention on the Black Jacks and 1869 Pictorials, which sell excellently. Some mint stamps are a good idea, too, and some of the $100-and-up stamps will show that you really mean business (pun intended). Except for air mails, special deliveries and ducks, back-of-the-book material does not sell that well for me. I suggest you tread lightly there if you are just beginning.

Stock the air mails complete, Zepps and all. My sales of Scott C1-6 always have been high. Perhaps it's because I'm careful to carry them in only the finest condition. They are very underrated, less than 5 percent of the printing total is extant today in XF or better, never hinged. The Maps, Lindbergh, China Clipper and Transport sets are always popular; so carry up to 10 each. For the balance of the airs up to Scott C32, carry five to 10 each. The lower the price, the more you carry. The Baby Zepp is another constant mover; keep at least five on hand.

I suggest keeping only two or three each of the Scott E14-23 Special Deliveries. Have some of the earlier ones in stock. However, don't worry about all of them. One or two Merry Widows (Scott E7) also are a must. Ducks are in great demand right now. You'll do well with them. Go for two or more each of the ones that sell for up to $50 each. Stock one each of the others.

While plate blocks are not as popular as they once were, you will be asked for them. Whether to carry them is up to you. As collector interest dwindled in the early '80s, I gave mine up because of little demand. Someday they may be popular again. If you stock them, have at least three each from Scott 702 to date of the ones that sell for up to $10 each. For the remainder, be 80 percent complete with one each.

The same formula applies to airmails. Three each of ones that sell for up to $10 each, for the remainder be 80 percent complete with one each. I strongly recommend that you forget about carrying mint sheets because of the tremendous inventory costs for the new dealer.

However, just having stock is not the same as knowing it. There are countless opportunities to make money by purchasing sleepers, stamps that are undervalued or misidentified by the seller. As a professional, you'll have to decide where the ethical line is. You might pay an unknowledgeable collector more than he asks for an undervalued stamp and be pleased to have the bargain if a dealer offers you the same stamp for the same price. By definition, a dealer is an expert who is responsible for looking out for him or herself.

You also may end up with sleepers that are a surprise to you. My greatest pleasure in philately comes from looking for sleepers as I break down and catalog collections and accumulations that I've just bought. The main reason for this jubilation is the philatelic education I receive. As I plunge into my Scott U.S. catalog, I'm in bliss as I track elusive rarities. I also get an on-going refresher in stamp identification.

I once found a Scott 21, in exceptionally fine condition, photographed and identified by a major auction house as a 23. I knew what I had found, and the Philatelic Foundation's expertising committee concurred. Another time I found the elusive "C" grill, Scott 83, which was sold to me by another dealer as a common No. 65. The point is that you will reap rewards from being informed and from constantly learning.

Once your education has begun and you've built your stock, you still have to price your stamps correctly to make your business profitable. Correct pricing starts with being aware of your overhead. That is one area where your accountant is particularly valuable. The month-to-month costs of doing business can kill you if you fail to allow for all of them.

Rent, utilities, taxes (except for income tax), advertising, professional fees, supplies, printing, postage, depreciation, your salary and bank fees all are part of stamp-dealer overhead for practical purposes. Add them together, and any other costs of staying in business, and divide your total by gross sales to determine overhead as a percent of sales. If it cost you $50,000 to do business and you have $100,000 in sales for the same period, your overhead is 50 percent. That is to say, 50 cents of every dollar of revenue is spent when you make the sale.

Some overhead, such as rent, is fixed. Some, like postage and printing, is variable. In other words, some expenses remain the same each month, and others vary with volume of business. Cover your fixed costs first. Then make sure your revenue goes up faster than your variable costs plus the costs of the goods you're selling. Profit is what's left over after overhead and cost of goods sold are covered. Your company is operating in the hole each month until you have made enough sales for the cash taken in to cover overhead and costs of goods sold.

Your salary is the most important overhead item. Let's say that with a spouse and two children, you want to have at least $30,000 a year income. That leaves $20,000 a year for remaining overhead, and you have a situation where you must go out and buy your stamps at exactly one-half their selling price just to eke out a living.

There are two ways to improve the situation. The first is to cut your overhead. If you are renting a store in a prime location, perhaps a mall, consider a new spot with lower rent. You can increase your salary by cutting every overhead item except your advertising budget. Cutting advertising will cut sales and dig you further and further into a hole. A second way to improve salary is to increase sales with innovative pricing or promotions.

Here are a couple of examples. You trim $5,000 off rent by moving. Overhead, less salary now is $15,000. You pared basic overhead from $20,000 to $15,000 a year, or 25 percent. The effect is to increase your salary from $30,000 to $35,000, which amounts to 16.7 percent.

Let's say you also increase sales by 50 percent, from $100,000 to $150,000 a year, by expanding your product base and establishing mail-bid sales. You save $5,000 with the move, and you pick up additional advertising, printing and other expenses that total $5,000 because of the costs of the new operation. You still have $20,000 basic overhead. Cost of the stock still is 50 percent of selling price, or $75,000 on $150,000 in sales. Basic overhead of $20,000 combined with $75,000 cost of goods sold amounts to $95,000. Your salary can rise from $30,000 to $55,000, or 83 percent. Total overhead still is 50 percent.

However, these examples make a best-case assumption that you can sell every item for twice what you pay for it, or a 100 percent markup, and that you're taking all your profit out of the business as salary, rather than reinvesting part of it into increasing the size of your business. Now, take the same conditions we've just discussed, except keep your salary constant at $30,000. You decrease your rent by $5,000, increase your sales to $150,000 and increase costs of selling by $5,000. You have $30,000 salary, $20,000 basic overhead and $75,000 cost of goods sold. Those total $125,000, against $150,000 in sales revenue. That leaves $25,000 to invest in your business by adding inventory or increasing advertising and promotion.

Still, though, we've been assuming you can sell every item for twice what you paid for it to keep the illustration simple. If you sell albums and supplies, you buy from distributors at 40 percent of retail. That means you pay $6 for an item you sell for $10 (assuming you don't have to discount to meet competition). Instead of selling for a 100 percent markup over cost, you're selling for 67 percent. And what about some of the blue-chip stamps? You may be glad to buy a stamp for $1,000 and resell it quickly for $1,300. That's a 30 percent markup.

Using our example above, a more realistic situation for your business is to say you're going to take $30,000 a year salary and invest $5,000 in increasing the value or size of the business. You also decide to allow for a lower markup than 100 percent. Now, this is the picture: $150,000 sales that breaks down into $95,000 cost of goods sold; $30,000 salary; $5,000 investment in company; $20,000 basic overhead. Every item has to be marked up 58 percent *on the average* for your business to stay the course. In other words, $150,000 is 58 percent greater than $95,000.

Now, when you sell $10 worth of supplies that cost you $6, you're making 9 percent more than your average markup. If you sell supplies that cost you $600 for $1,000 (a 67 percent markup), you can sell stamps that cost you $670 for $1,000 (a 49 percent markup) and keep your 58 percent average markup. With this example, your total overhead (salary, investment in the company and basic overhead) now is $55,000, or 37 percent of sales.

To be a successful stamp dealer, you constantly must think mark-up – the percentage you must add to the cost of each item to cover your costs and provide a profit when you make a sale.

In the example we've been using, your salary is an operating expense, and the $5,000 that you invest in the business amounts to the net profit of the company. That means your business is making 3.3 percent of sales as profit *before income taxes*. The lower your markup, the lower your profit percentage is going to be, and the more volume of sales you're going to have to make to keep your salary constant.

If you are running a successful business with less than 10 percent of sales as before-income-tax profit, you're a skillful businessman. You probably are doing a large volume of sales, too. If you're starting a business, your volume will be low (unless you buy a going company). You will be wise to plan on making at least a 10 percent profit. It's common for large, profitable stamp companies to make 20 percent and more.

An alternative to thinking in terms of markup, is to consider your *markon*. It is your gross profit on selling price, or the difference between your cost for an item and the amount you sell it for. (Your net profit, or operating income before income taxes, is the amount that is obtained by deducting all the expenses of your business from all the revenue.) To use the last example above, we sell for $150,000 stamps and supplies that cost us $95,000. The markup is 58 percent. However, the markon, or profit on selling price, is 36.6 percent. So I know in advance that I must make 36.6 cents on each dollar of gross sales to cover my basic overhead and salary and make the investment I plan to increase the size of my business.

Armed with this information I now know that a set of stamps I intend to sell for $20 had better not cost me more than $12.66. Preferably, I'll be able to get them for less. I said earlier that in this business the money is made by buying right, not by selling. If I am able to purchase this mythical set for $10 instead $12.66, I just "made" $2.66.

Overhead can eat you alive if you let it. Depend on your accountant to keep tabs on your financial house and to report any trouble spots. (At the same time, don't allow accounting and legal fees to become a major overhead item!)

One cost that can strangle you is carrying inventory. Earlier, I mentioned the three-month system of turning inventory. It is important to consider again here because your bank loan carries a hefty finance charge. If, for example, that rate is 12 percent, it makes the $10,000 collection you just bought end up costing you over $11,000 in one year when you take the front-loaded finance charges into account. This means you have added 10 percent to your overhead on that collection.

The moral is to avoid taking out a 12-month note on the purchase of a collection unless you're certain you're going to make a lot of money on the collection. Plan to at least double your money on it, or pass it by.

The same basic strategy is applicable to the purchase of inventory. If you're not going to resell it reasonably quickly, you've overpaid at almost any price. What good is it to spend $100 on something that *should* sell for $200 or $300 if it is only going to sit in your stockbook gathering dust while it awaits a buyer? I'd rather have 10 items that cost $10 each and sell them quickly for $15 each. I've turned over stock and made a one-third markon. Now I've got $150 to invest in some more good items that I can move fast.

Your inventory should completely turn over each three months, or at least four times a year. Popular items such as the Farleys, Famous Americans and similar material should be in a constant state of turnover. The key is that you don't ever want to purchase more than a three-month supply of anything. If your sales history suggests that you turn over 20 sets of Famous Americans every three months then don't purchase 40 sets unless: (1) the price is at least 25 percent less than you paid the last time, and (2) you have ample cash to spend on the extra 20 sets. You must answer yes to both questions to make this the only exception to your "don't ever buy more than a three-month supply rule."

Suppose that you are accustomed to spending $16 each for fine to very fine, never hinged sets of Famous Americans. You normally sell them for $24 each. You are given an opportunity to buy 40 sets at $12 each in a cash deal. The price gives you the required 25 percent minimum cost savings, and you have the extra money in your checking account to handle the transaction. You have thus met both requirements of your supply rule. Looking at the math, you have spent only an extra $160 since to buy 20 sets you would have spend $320 at your regular cost. Your 40 set deal needed a $480 outlay.

Now you have some options to consider. You can go with the original game plan of selling your usual 20 sets in three months at your regular $24 price, or you can offer the sets as an inducement, by offering "a nice set of fine to very fine, never hinged Famous Americans at one-third off our regular low price." This type of offering, a set of Famous Americans at $18, in conjunction with a $50 purchase from your price list will often result in double turnover, or turnover of the promotional item and moving some of your regular stock as well.

In this illustration, you net the same one-third markon: regular $24 selling price against a $16 cost, or special $18 selling price against a $12 cost. If you can arrange the turnover of the 40 sets in the same three-month period, you will find that your dollar profits also are higher. By selling 40 sets at the $18 price, you've grossed a profit of $240. The turnover of 20 sets at the regular price realizes a gross profit of $160. You now have more dollars with which to buy more inventory.

Realize early in your professional philatelic career that turnover is job No. 1 and that idle stock costs you tremendously. Who is wiser, the dealer who picked up the $100 item based on hope alone or the individual who made the fortuitous Famous American purchase? Stock that sits costs you money – always. That money could be spent over and over again, as we've illustrated, on bonafide good stock that will turn over. Even if that money were in a passbook savings account, it would earn several percent more a year than it does in your dusty stockbook.

Here's another bitter pill to swallow. Sell dead inventory at any cost. Even if you must do so at a loss, you'll be putting money into good material that, by turning over, will repay the loss quickly. If you still can't dispose of those dogs after several price cuts, consider auctioning them off. Your existence depends on turnover. I worry if 25 percent of my stock is going nowhere, even though 75 percent is flying out of my stockbooks. I'm greedy. I want it all to move, and you need to work for that, too. The smart dealer will swallow his losses, and his pride, and put that money into bigger and better things.

There are other ways to make money. We'll talk about them next.

Chapter 6
Business Builders

I once considered producing price lists, which now are among my most pleasurable tasks, as unsure and as potentially unpleasant as blind dates. Getting a list out can be quite a painless and—once you have a system in place—really enjoyable adventure. Everyone has the ability to do it successfully because it is a simple three-step operation: counting, typing and pasting.

Planning is the key ingredient to any successful business operation. You must first decide on the type of price list you intend to publish and have an idea about the contents. Then, you must budget sufficient time to do a thorough job.

I publish two different lists: a master list and a periodic highlights list. The master list comes out twice yearly, usually in March and September. It primarily contains items that are easily replaceable, such as most of the commemoratives and perhaps 95 percent of the 20th century regular issues. All air mails are included. The grades are mostly fine-to-very fine, and there also is a nice selection of very fine and better stamps. I don't stock hinged stamps after Scott 701 and C15 because they simply don't sell.

My periodic price list is normally issued to highlight new acquisitions or close-outs. It is the one that I use predominately, often releasing it four to six times a year. In it, I can list whatever I want to move out at the time. I also sprinkle through it a healthy dose of regular stock items like popular sets, commemorative year sets, Farley issues, air mails and other quick movers. I feature one-of-a-kind offerings as well.

How detailed should your listings be? Again, that depends on the list you are issuing. In my master list I construct three columns per page and confine each listing to one line. This accommodates a lot of listings without appearing crammed. I can "spice up" the periodic list visually because I don't have to worry about listing as many items as in the master list. Here, I write up one or two columns per page and use as many lines as I need to pitch each item.

I recently made a mistake at auction and bought far too many sets of the U.S. 1928 Aeronautics issue. Fortunately, each set was clearly very fine or better, and I happened to buy them right. I candidly admitted my goof-up to my price list audience and offered the sets first-come, first-served at a price slightly lower than my regular price for a fine to very-fine set. You guessed it! I sold out in no time.

The main advantage to using the periodic price list is that you do not have to worry about carrying an in-depth stock of everything in your specialty. This is important for newer dealers on tight budgets. You choose the stamps you are going to list and have in greater depth than the rest of the stock on your master list. On one-of-a-kind items, customers usually will not balk at a refund check because you have already mentioned that the list is composed of unique items. The opposite is true of your master price list. You are expected to have a beyond-belief inventory of everything on it.

Regardless of which list you publish, you must indicate how long the prices are valid. My March master price list states that prices will be honored until Aug. 31 or the issuance of a new list, whichever comes first. Always use the "next list" disclaimer to protect yourself from price swings.

My summer periodic price list notes that "prices are valid until sold out, the issuance of my next list or when the kids go back to school, whichever comes first." How do you make your lists different from those of your competitors? One way is to inject mild humor. Most all of your customers have senses of humor.

Other ways are to include brief commentaries and illustrations. You might even consider featuring a regular column of philatelic information. For example, you could write a short piece on how the U.S. 1898 Trans-Mississippis were to have been bicolor until the Spanish-American War got in the way.

Monthly specials can be used successfully, especially within the master list. For example, your April special could be a set of Norse-Americans at half your regular price with an order for $100 or more. The possibilities are limited only by your imagination.

At times, I conduct a small contest and award a prize. Sometimes, I add a cartoon to the list. I do any philatelic thing I can think of to make my lists the exception to everyone else's.

By adopting some of these ideas and adding some of your own, you can create price lists that will be anticipated eagerly by your clients because the lists are interesting to read and perhaps even worth keeping. Even if only some clients order from a particular list, you'll also set yourself up for future sales by showing your name and wares frequently, which increases recognition of your business.

Now that we've decided on the type of list that's just right for you and your inventory, let's plan a time frame for preparing it for the printer.

Before writing your first price list, you must devote many hours to "market study." To be competitive, you must be aware of your competition. I use a columnar pad with six columns and a description space. I dutifully log the stamp or set and follow with prices from five of my competitors. The sixth column has my selling price. One could conceivably spend 40 or more hours just to get a good feel of prevailing U.S. stamp prices.

The actual layout, typing and paste-up should range from 10 to 15 hours depending on the type of list and depth of your stock. Whether to use a typewriter or computer is a personal choice. I have a wonderful typewriter with built-in dictionary, a self-correcting feature, and interchangeable printwheels, among other conveniences. I bought it several years ago before computers became as cheap and practical as they are today, and I continue to use it for price lists.

(I eventually purchased a computer that stores my inventory, mailing list, customer files and other pertinent data and is operated by one of my many capable offspring. Although I know how to use it, the children are more efficient and do a better job with it. You must evaluate your own position with the tools and equipment at hand. If you don't have a computer, I advise taking a course before you rush out to buy one.)

Which persons on your mailing list will get the price list? The answer comes from categorizing your customers. My No. 1 list is active clients who have spent at least $100 during the past six months. Smaller expenditures do not usually indicate the spending habits of serious collectors who eventually will be coming to you for rare classics. If I've added a new name to my mailing list recently and the expenditures have not yet reached the targeted amount, I keep the client on the No. 1 list and then act appropriately when six months is reached.

Customers are not locked into a particular category of mailing list, i.e. #1, #2, #3, #4. Review your list at least quarterly and weed out the ones who have been inactive for a year and a half.

Your No. 2 mailing list can be collectors who have ordered at least once during the past six months and whose purchases did not total $100.

Your No. 3 list might contain names of persons who requested your list during the previous 12 months but did not order. (Will they ever?) You also might include those who ordered in the past but have been inactive for the past six months.

Look at this last group carefully. Did they fail to order because of a temporary cash pinch? Have they found a new dealer who offers something you don't? Are they still collecting? Whatever the reason, follow up. It's probably cheaper to revive them than to find new customers.

When you're mailing to active customers and good prospects, always use first-class mail franked with commemoratives.

Last, are the people who asked for your list more than a year ago, who never ordered, and who have yet to respond to a follow-up effort. Privately, I call these so-called stamp collectors my "deceased file." About the only way that they could receive a mailing is if I have lists left over from improperly gauging response to some newly placed advertising. Then I may send at least 200 pieces to limit my investment to the cost of envelopes, bulk-rate stamps and final-effort coupons.

The coupons are valid for 60 days and are rubber stamped with appropriate expiration dates. I use a form letter to advise the prospect that this is my final effort. If there is no response, I declare the individual philatelically dead. I keep the customer card in a separate file box and check it as each new inquiry for a price list comes in. You'd be surprised at how many people ask for a list once a year or so. Sometimes they even ask several times a year. I once sent the lists, hoping the people would order. I found out the hard way, however, that they were only list collectors and weren't even worth the cost of third-class postage for repeat lists.

Bulk-rate permits are not that expensive, and third-class mail is useful for many things besides price lists. When you send small gifts to active clients at year's end, you might mail bulk in November and make some nice savings. Or you may want to let customers and prospective clients know you're coming to a show in their area. Use bulk-rate notices about three weeks ahead. There are many other ways to save money mailing, too. Always be open to the possibilities.

Speaking of using stamps on your mailing, a few otherwise sane individuals will castigate you for not using a colorful array of older commemoratives. Once in a while these nit pickers spew their venom through letters in the philatelic press. One wonders why editors choose to print such useless verbiage. Perhaps there are no other important philatelic matters to discuss at that time. I believe the offering inside is more important than the postage used to convey it. There is absolutely nothing wrong with using a modern, single commemorative, rather than five or six older ones, and it saves you a lot of time.

Whether your labels are computer generated or typed and photocopied onto label stock, you'll benefit from information on them identifying your customers. The system that I use is simple and effective. The upper right hand corner of the label is my ID area.

For a collector who requested my list from a *Stamp Collector* newspaper classified ad during June 1995, the printed area would read 01XSCC0695. The 01 identifies the list number, or category, that has been assigned to the client. All new inquiries are given 01 status from the beginning and are moved down the scale from 02 to 04 as time dictates. The X tells me this is a new prospect without a six-month customer history. I use the other letters of the alphabet to assist me in identifying the customer's primary buying habits. H indicates this individual is a postal history buff. W means a specialty in the U.S. Washington-Franklin definitives. The remaining letters are used for a host of other collecting interests.

The best part about adopting such a system is that you are not limited to just one interest category. Your customer might be active in many fields. To separate the buying habits from the remainder of my label code, I use a Q when there's more than one interest area. For example, if this collector subsequently orders air mails and special delivery stamps, the label will read 01AEQSCC0695.

Getting back to our original example, we now continue with the source data. SCC refers to a *Stamp Collector* classified ad. I would have used SCD to identify a display ad. The 0695 dates the initial customer contact as June 1995. The source data is very important. In time, you'll be able to see what publications are more effective for you and at what times of the year your ads pull better.

I invest most of my advertising budget seeking requests for my price list. If I did run display ads offering priced items for sale, I would encode the label SCP to show the customer bought from a *Stamp Collector* newspaper ad with priced stamps for sale.

In the beginning, you must decide who gets your list and when. You may want to reward your 01 list for past loyalty by mailing their lists out a week or so ahead of everybody else. Of course, this will exclude your new prospects, the X designees. If you've just purchased some nice back-of-the-book stamps, you probably will want to send a special mailing to customers who buy that kind of material.

The next step is composing the list. After costly experimenting, I settled on two-sided 8½ x11-inch offset-printed sheets for my periodic lists. Five 20-pound bond sheets and a No. 10 envelope weigh one ounce, with no room for a stuffer or return envelope. I use a different pastel color for each mailing. Studies have shown response rates are higher for mailing pieces on colored paper than for those with white paper. Color also helps collectors distinguish your list from others. Some of my favorites are beige, yellow, blue, green, pink and gray. I suggest that you avoid using bold, bright colors, which offend some people's eyes.

When you are ready to compose your list, what you don't want to do is simply to turn on your computer and start banging away, top to bottom, side to side. If you don't have a program that automatically provides columns or if you're using a typewriter, divide the number of columns desired into the total number of characters across to get the number of characters available per column for each line. Leaving two characters between each column will allow space for a line separating the columns. By measuring type height and doing an inch on some scrap paper, you'll quickly determine how many lines will fit on your page.

Before you sit down at the keyboard, talk to your printer if your computer or typewriter produces only regular-size type. The printer can save you money by photographically reducing your original copy. If you provide him or her with enough steady business, your printer even may waive the small fees for work like reducing copy and incorporating logos.

With my typewriter, I start with 12x16-inch paper and type top to bottom, side to side, leaving one-fourth- to three-eighths-inch margins all around for the grippers on the printing press. I'm also careful to avoid smudges and marks I don't want on the finished piece. Whatever appears on my camera-ready copy is printed. My printer reduces the page to fit 8½ x11-inch paper. I get a nifty looking piece with just the right amount of "white space" to make it readable. I also get 50 percent more copy on each page than I would without the reduction. That translates into many more items offered to customers for the same amount of postage. And the more I offer, the higher my sales are likely to be.

If a one-third reduction produces smaller type than you want on the finished product, use 11x14-inch sheets and having them reduced by 25 percent. Your finished 8½ x11-inch product will yield a full one-third more copy. Whatever size you choose, be sure your piece will be readable. Customer eyestrain will work against you, no matter how much you save on postage.

Keep your lists consistent in size and type and headline style. You will build an identity that will cause your customers to become eager to search for new stamps each time they see your mail. Customers also will perceive you unconsciously as a predictable, reliable dealer and will feel more comfortable about ordering. Consistency will help you and your printer, too. As you two get into a groove, you are more likely to get what you want each time without confusion.

Be sure your list is two-sided. I can't tell you of the number of lists I've received that have been printed on one side of the sheet only. I wonder if those dealers know that it is cheaper to print up three sheets that are two-sided as opposed to six of the one-sided variety, not to mention cutting their postage in half?

There are other costs to consider, too. Some, like printing overruns, are hidden. The printing process requires latitude, and the flexibility is at the printers end. They must print at least as many pieces as you order and customarily may print up to 10 percent more. Any extras can be a bonus business-builder for you. Give your printer a written order with the quantity desired. State on the order that you won't pay for overruns of any number, as well as for *any* other items or services not on the order, unless they are authorized in advance by you in writing.

Some services to consider at the time you order are paste-up, collating, folding, stapling and envelope stuffing. One of the advantages of having a large family is that I get most of those services for much less by hiring children and keep the money in the family. As for paste-up, if you use logos, illustrations or headlines, do the pasting yourself.

Get at least three estimates, as you would in other situations. If two prices are within 10 percent of each other, go with the printer who impresses you as being the easiest to work with.

MAIL-BID SALES AND MAIL AUCTIONS

There is a difference!

A mail auction awards the lot to the highest bidder at one advance over the second highest bid. There is only one of each lot. States such as New York further require by law that if the word "auction" is used, public bidding from a floor with an auctioneer be included.

The mail-bid sale usually finds each lot going to the highest bidder at the exact price bid. Quite often, multiples of each lot are available, and just as frequently they are all sold to different bidders at different prices. For example, let us say that the dealer has four sets of a certain issue, all alike in grade. He only lists one set and receives several bids. The top four bids are $14, $12.50, $12 and $11. Since he paid only $8 each, he decides to ship all four sets out to the four different bidders at the prices they bid. Worse yet, he has a fifth bid for $10.50 and still can buy another set for $8. He does so and sends this out as well.

I firmly believe it is unethical to sell five lots of stamps to five customers, each of whom thinks he or she is the highest bidder for a single advertised lot. I don't do business that way, and I recommend you avoid it.

In a mail auction, the correct way to treat bids is for each lot to be awarded to the highest bidder at one advance over the second highest bid. In this case one lot should go to the highest bidder at $13. No other lots are sold to anyone else.

In a mail-bid sale, only one lot should be awarded and it is invoiced at $14, which is in accordance with the terms of all lots being sold to the highest bidder. What separates the mail-bid sale from the mail-bid auction are the key words "at one advance over the second highest bid."

It goes without saying that your business benefits from treating all customers fairly and honestly. If the mail-bid sale dealer in our illustration had four identical lots, he should have listed them as such or made a wholesale offering of three sets to encourage dealer bids. I prefer to conduct only mail auctions and every aspect is as if it were an auction with bidding from the floor. Satisfied bidders who receive lots at nice savings from their bids are long-term, steady customers.

Before you begin to hold your own sales, you must get consignments. There is no shortcut for experience. You must be known in the philatelic world to get decent material. Once you have established your presence and have decided that mail auctions are for you, prepare that initial advertisement seeking consignments. Your own retail customers might very well surprise you as an untapped source for good consignment material. Everyone has duplicate or unwanted stamps to dispose of. Best of all, many of your customers will take payment in stamps from your inventory. This can make mail auctions even more profitable.

Another tip in planning consignments is to have your second sale booked, have enough material on hand to run the second sale without worrying about where the lots are going to come from. Be working on the third sale when you mail out the first, etc. Finally, establish terms and conditions for bidders and consignors.

These are the conditions of sale that I used in a recent mail auction:

1. Our mail auctions treat your high bid the same way you might expect in a public auction. Each lot sells for one advance over the second highest bid. For example, you bid $60 on a lot that you need. Our second highest recorded bid is $40. You are awarded the lot at $42.

2. Payment is by check or money order within five days of receipt of our invoice. You also may use your Visa or MasterCard. Be sure to say at the time you place your bids how you want to pay.

3. All forwarding charges are in addition to your winning bid(s). NJ residents also pay 6 percent sales tax. NJ dealers, send your exemption certificate.

4. All lots are sold as genuine and as described, unless marked "as-is." Any incorrectly described lot may be returned in the same condition as received within five days of receipt.

These lots are NOT RETURNABLE under any circumstances: (a) any lot sold "as-is," (b) any lot containing 10 or more items, (c) any illustrated or photocopied lot for reasons of centering, perforations or cancellation, (d) any lot examined before the sale, (e) any lot received by us after 14 days from the closing date (except lots covered in the next paragraph).

5. Any lot may be sent to The Philatelic Foundation for expertising, provided that we receive your written notice of intent within 14 days of the closing date. The sending of any lot(s) to the Foundation does not in any way relieve you of your obligation to pay for such lot(s) in accordance with our terms. If, for any reason, the Foundation finds the lot is not as described by us, we will accept the return for prompt refund including the expertising costs.

6. We reserve the right to withdraw any lot or to group two or more lots together. Bid by lot number, please.

7. Until paid for in full, all lots remain the property of Peter Mosiondz, Jr., on behalf of the seller.

8. We charge only a 20 percent seller's commission. There is NO BUYER'S FEE of any kind.

9. The placing of any bid(s) constitutes full acceptance of the foregoing conditions of sale.

GOOD LUCK AND THANKS FOR YOUR PARTICIPATION!

Bidding intervals:

Bids   Advance

Up to $20	$ 1
$22 to $48	2
$50 to $95	5
$100 to $290	10
$300 to $775	25
$800 to $1950	50
$2,000 and up	5%

I then plead for bids in even dollar amounts, cautioning that bids received in odd amounts or otherwise not conforming to our posted intervals will be reduced accordingly. The inevitable happens. Dozens of bid sheets are received that do not conform.

Next, I advise that photocopies of any lot not illustrated are available for 25 cents a lot and an addressed, stamped envelope, if I receive the request at least seven days before the sale date. Following this is a tentative schedule for the next five or six sales and a paragraph advising that all lots are available for inspection at my office.

Then comes my bid sheet. Nothing fancy about this. You've seen dozens of them probably. Since I accept charge cards, I feature this prominently and allocate enough room for customers to provide me with the vital facts for the sale: name, address, phone number and references.

I have found it advisable to publish consignment terms at the end of the sale, after the last lot. A lead-in like "Turn Those Unwanted Stamps Into Cash" is effective.

I then begin my pitch with "The type of material that you see in this catalog is basically what we need." Because I am known as a dealer in U.S. stamps, I point out that I would not be a logical candidate for handling foreign stamps.

I then offer my instructions for packaging and mailing the consignment: Prepare the lots by putting each in a glassine envelope. Then send them to me in an outer envelope, listing pertinent data — such as Scott catalog number(s), grade and reserve price (if any) — by lot.

Next, I state my commission rate of a flat 20 percent of selling price (10 percent if $20,000 or more is sold for the seller in the same sale). I then note that if, in my opinion, a certificate of authenticity is needed to sell an item, I will submit the item to The Philatelic Foundation and invoice the consignor's account for the certificate costs. There are no other charges. The costs of insurance, advertising, listing and promotion are included in our commission rate.

Settlement is discussed next, with the promise that all checks will be mailed 45 days after the closing date. Consignors are told not to request payment any sooner and that my record of paying everyone as promised is 100 percent. I also note that all material is fully insured while under my care. The consignor is asked to furnish a packing list in duplicate, one copy of which will be returned along with any comments, discrepancies in grading, cancellation identification or usage.

Closing this portion I say, "By consigning material to us you are pledging that you are the lawful owner of the material and that you will pay any costs incurred by us, and hold us harmless from any cost or guilt in the event of legal action." When I return the duplicate of the packing list, I also enclose my consignment contract in duplicate. The consignor signs and returns the original.

Reserve pricing, the minimum acceptable to the consignor excluding the auctioneer's commission, is a touchy subject. I prefer to avoid reserve prices. I accept them only for stamps or sets that are expected to realize $500 or more. One of my consignors once put a reserve price on a set of Famous Americans, the height of philatelic folly. Anyone can buy a set for $25 or less today. It is not a scarce item. Let your consignors know you will not sell them out for the sake of a modest commission.

I tell my consignors that on stamps (sets) valued at under $100, I will not accept bids of less than 70 percent retail (i.e. my interpretation of retail based on 27 years experience). On stamps (sets) valued at $100 and higher, I will not accept bids of less than 80 percent retail. Note: I do not charge a buyer's fee. If I did then the above percent of retail would be 60 and 70 respectively.

When you do take a reserve on an appropriate set, be sure your consignor knows that if the lot is unsold you will invoice your commission fee of the reserve.

When mailing your list, use first class mail and post it 21 days before the closing date. Allowing for delivery time, you are targeting the list to be in your bidder's hands 18 days before the sale date. I've found this is the timing that produces the best response.

When your mailing list grows to at least 2,000 and you are producing thick, lavish catalogs, you may want to go to bulk-rate mail. Then, you will have to mail six to seven weeks before the sale date.

Other marketing considerations you'll want to consider for auctions and mail-bid sales include:

• Will you rent names? *Stamp Collector* newspaper is an excellent source of current collectors who buy by mail. *Stamp Collector* rents a minimum of 5,000 names at a time.

- What will your commission be?
- Will you have illustrations? A picture is worth a thousand words — not to mention dozens of extra bid sheets.
- Will you accept credit cards? The smart dealer does and sees the result as increased sales and profits.
- How and where will you advertise for bidders and consignors?
- Will you offer a prices realized list? I suggest you provide a copy free of charge to all successful bidders and to every consignor.

Running a mail auction requires hard work. It also is work that will pay off handsomely in the end.

SPECIAL OFFERS

Besides featuring slow-moving items in your periodic price list, you may decide to gear up a special-offers bulletin. I use an 8½ x 11-inch sheet, tri-folding it into a self-mailer with my return address, a stamp and the address of the customer on one-third of the second side. I show an expiration date for the special prices and use the AIDA approach to copy writing that I explained in the advertising chapter.

The special-offers bulletin also is a perfect place to sell special purchases you may have made. Remember those Baby Zepps in the chapter on advertising? This is a good way to move some of them out at a profit and to benefit your customers in a way that makes them more loyal to you.

LAY-AWAYS

Don't underestimate the power of lay-aways as business builders. Spell out your terms in a clear and friendly manner. Most collectors are not going to share intimate details of their financial situations with you. A customer may be embarrassed to tell you he or she is running on empty, or close to it, right now, although money will be more plentiful in a month or two.

I like to say,"Lay-aways are cordially invited. Just send one-third with your order, another third in 30 days and the final third 30 days after that. It's that easy, and you'll get those stamps that you really want." This approach has led to many sales I might not have gotten. I have a $100 minimum on layaways.

I avoid saying things like, "Layaways tailored to your individual needs." Just about anyone who is in a temporary bind can handle a sensible purchase over a 60-day period. Avoid the pitfall of playing financial advisor by customizing lay-aways. Assuming responsibility for your customers' budgeting is an easy way to accept blame for their mistakes and to lose them as customers.

The neatest feature about handling lay-aways is that you get business from people who, unable to discipline themselves otherwise, will faithfully adhere to payment schedules and spend money with you that would have gone to other stamp dealers or hobbies.

ADVERTISING SPECIALTIES

One of the greatest giveaways I ever had was a little coupon-clipping device imprinted with my name, address, phone number and specialty. My customers loved them because they were handy for cutting articles and ads from stamp papers. Such items are called advertising specialties because they are ways of reminding people often about your business. Effective ad specialties need to be used often, preferably daily. The objective is to keep your products and services fresh in collectors' minds.

As elementary as it sounds, another great item for me that I still give away is a retractable ball-point pen with my name and slogan. I've given away thousands over the years. Of course I'm not a philanthropist. These products have a job to do. They are subliminal sales boosters, or "silent salesmen" as I call them.

Other suitable specialties include calendars, monthly planners, bookmarks and pocket stock books. A glance at your Yellow Pages under the heading of Advertising Specialties should reveal some good sources. You'll find others advertised in *The Stamp Wholesaler* newspaper. Your printer also may have suggestions like memo pads. They are good sales boosters.

Another way you can use more substantial specialties like pocket stock books is to offer them free to a customer when a collector orders from your list within, say, two weeks of receipt or when a customer orders at least $50 worth from a particular list. If a stock book that retails for $5 costs you $2.50, you can give a customer ordering $50 worth of stamps a 10 percent discount that only costs you 5 percent.

You get double use from specialty items you use as premiums. They boost sales when they are ordered, and they continue to remind the customer that you offer savings and good deals. Use premiums only with full-price offers as a rule. When you send out a special-price bulletin, the special prices are the "premiums."

COUPONS

I also like to use $1 coupons, with qualifications, to entice new accounts. The coupons are good on orders of $10 or more and are valid only for 30 days after the day I make my mailing. This date is rubber stamped on each coupon leaving my office. The reasoning is the same as for premiums. Everyone likes a freebie. The $10 requirement is small enough to prompt most collectors to place trial orders. The 30-day cut-off time inspires action on the recipient's part. Your purpose with the coupon is to encourage new clients to give your service a try. Be confident that once the trial order is placed, you'll see plenty of repeat orders.

Whether you are selling through mail auctions and mail-bid sales, special offers, lay-aways or with advertising specialties and premiums, the rule is the same. Be innovative to be successful.

Chapter 7
Tools and Equipment

Just as plumbers carry their wrenches and torches, stamp dealers also need tools. Two of my "best friends" are both Showgard brand items. I've had Showgard's No. 607 clear perforation gauge for years, and I am never without my No. 902 pointed-tip professional tongs.

My black-glass watermark dish and fluid are always within reach on my desk, too. Expert use of a watermark tray not only helps identify stamps, but enables one to spot flaws and repairs in them as well. The book, *How to Detect Damaged, Altered, & Repaired Stamps,* by Paul Schmid, also is a must.

I depend heavily on two magnifiers, each of which has its own task. My 4-power lens is the workhorse. It's used for the routine examination of a couple of hundred stamps daily. It's invaluable for checking perforations and overall appearance of stamps. It also helps me to spot repairs and other problem areas that might go undetected by the naked eye.

I grab my 10X glass whenever I am checking grills or looking for transfer varieties and the like. It also makes the chore of identifying those troublesome 2-cent Washingtons quite a bit more palatable. In fact, every important find or discovery I have made has involved my trusty old 10X.

A tool that is often overlooked by aspiring dealers, and that can make you as much money as it has made me, is the UV (ultraviolet) light. One of these days, U.S. "tagged" stamps will rightfully come into their own. The dealer who is looking for them now and who recognizes the rarities that are out there and stockpiles them will reap a future reward. I recommend a dual-power UV light that supplies both long- and short-wave illumination. The short-wave will detect phosphorescent tagging on U.S. issues; the long-wave will aid you with foreign stamps. The Raytech LS-4 and LS-7 are excellent models. When you work with ultraviolet lights, be extremely careful not to look into them even though they are the only lights on at the time.

They can damage your eyes.

When you are seated at your desk at other times, you will want an excellent light source to make your work more pleasant and efficient. I position my desk so that I take full advantage of the morning sun as its rays fall over my left shoulder. A floor lamp with a 50-100-150-watt incandescent bulb is positioned just to my right rear. My 100-watt desk lamp throws off plenty of soft-white incandescent light when beckoned. Halogen lighting, which is a relatively new source, creates the most natural illumination. My tests have been successful enough to make me seriously think of changing over soon.

Some may choose fluorescent lighting. I find most of it makes stamps and covers look unnatural, and I recommend avoiding it.

When it comes to storing stock, there are several ways to go. After trying about all the stock pages available, I have been using Hagner one-sided black pages in various row configurations for years. I use them for everything except panes, which I keep in old-fashioned glassine mint-sheet files. When I'm planning to work a show, I slip my Hagner pages into inert Mylar sheet protectors. This preventive medicine all but eliminates the sleight-of-hand artists who prey on distracted dealers at shows.

I once was an advocate of the so-called "dealer sales sheets," those 5½ x 8½-inch white or yellow pages with clear pockets on printed backgrounds or see-through pockets, depending on one's preference. One problem with these pages is that the pocket eventually loosens at the bottom, allowing stamps to slide out.

Stockbooks with old-fashioned Manila pockets are used by many dealers. I don't like the way stamps slide and move about in the relatively loose pockets.

When I ship stamps, I pack them in glassines. The No. 3 size is perfect for singles and most sets. You'll need some larger sizes, too, for items like souvenir sheets and covers.

I created a nice rubber stamp that I use for my glassines. This is what it looks like:

U.S. SCOTT #_____ PRICE_____

NH LH H USED AVG F F-VF VF XF SUP

IF IT'S U.S. STAMPS, PETE CAN'T BE BEAT!

I circle the condition and grade, then enter the Scott catalog number and price.

My slogan is also there. My philatelic mentor, Herman "Pat" Herst, Jr., had a similar phrase. It went: "If It's U.S.A. Stamps, See Herst First." I was thinking out loud one day to a friend about how nice it would be if I could come up with something equally as catching. A week later, a small package arrived. It contained a rubber stamp, which I still use today, that says: "If It's U.S. Stamps, Pete Can't Be Beat!"

Another one of my favorite rubber stamps is: "Better U.S. Stamps for Sale?/ We Eagerly Purchase Such Material/ Or Accept on Consignment for Our/ Popular Mail Auctions or Direct Sales." It brings in some nice material. I have many rubber stamps on the swivel racks on my desk. Each has its own purpose, and all have one aspect in common—they all do a magnificent job of self-promotion.

Earlier, I presented a basic library for every dealer. Other books you add to it will depend on your specialty. Your *working* philatelic library is one of your most important tools. Note, however, that even if you have every philatelic book ever printed, your philatelic knowledge will not increase if you do not read the books.

Here are some, not all, of the books that are on my shelves. If you are a U.S. specialist, you probably will want these as a minimum:

Scott U.S. Specialized Catalogue.

Scott-Micarelli Manual and Identification Guide to the Regular Issues 1847-1934.

The American Stampless Cover Catalogue (two volumes).

Steve Datz's *U.S. Errors (latest edition).*

Durland's Plate Number Catalogue.

The United States Postage Stamps of the 19th Century (three volumes) by Lester G. Brookman.

The four-volume set of Max Johl books.

Fundamentals of Philately by L.N. & M. Williams.

U.S. Cancellations 1845-1869 by Skinner & Eno.

19th Century United States Fancy Cancellations by Herman Herst, Jr.

Chase's *Classic United States Stamps 1845-1869.*

Counterfeit Kansas-Nebraska Overprints on 1922-34 Issue (an APS handbook).

The Bank Note Issues of United States Stamps 1870-1893 by Lester G. Brookman.

United States Grills by William L. Stevenson (and, in the same Triad Publications handbook, *Notes on the Grilled Issues of the United States* by Lester G. Brookman).

A Census of United States Classic Plate Blocks by John C. Chapin.

United States Coil Issues 1906-1938 by Martin A. Armstrong.

U.S. Definitive Series 1922-1938 by Martin A. Armstrong.

Washington-Franklins 1908-1921 by Martin A. Armstrong.

Foundations of Philately by Winthrop S. Boggs.

Color in Philately by Roy H. White.

Printing Postage Stamps by Line Engraving by James H. Baster.

Opinions I, II, III, IV, V and VI, published by the Philatelic Foundation.

The Stamp Specialist, 20 volumes published 1939-1948 by H.L. Lindquist.

Discovering U.S. Rotary Booklet Pane Varieties 1926-1978 by Bruce H. Mosher.

How to Detect Damaged, Altered, & Repaired Stamps, Paul Schmid's masterpiece.

Postage Stamps in the Making by F.J. Melville.

Baker's *U.S. Classics.*

U.S. Philatelic Miscellany by Susan MacDonald.

This is Philately, three-volume encyclopedia by Kenneth Wood.

The American Philatelic Congress books.

Every Pat Herst book, especially *Nassau Street*, which I've read more than 20 times already.

The Philatelic Foundation *Bulletins* and *Analysis Leaflets* are of prime value and are available to PF contributors.

The above list is not intended to be complete or gospel. You'll add or delete according to your own specialty. The dealer in more modern material may have no need for the three-volume Brookman classic on 19th century U.S. and its expensive price tag.

You will see books and handbooks come up at auction quite frequently. Avail yourself of this magnificent means of adding to your library. Auction catalogs and resulting prices realized should be saved, especially the Siegel sales if you handle U.S. stamps. Subscribe to the price lists of the leading philatelic literature dealers.

What do you do with all these books? You read them. You read them again. You continually study them. It is an on-going course in philatelic self-education. In philately, one can never acquire enough knowledge, or happen to wake up one morning knowing everything there is to know about stamps.

There is another piece of equipment every dealer should have: a safe. This is especially so for store owners. Check with the APS Insurance Plan manager for the recommended type. When I had my store, the minimum acceptable rating was an ERTL-15. Safes are rated on their burglary-resistant features and the thickness of their steel walls. The bolts come into play also, as do fire-resistant properties. Insurance under the APS dealer plan requires an approved safe if the desired coverage is to be over $50,000, a figure easily surpassed by every full-time dealer.

A suitable cash register is another store necessity. Look for one that allows you to program in transactions like stamp, cover, supplies and literature sales. The more useful data you can gather, the better. You need to know exactly what you are selling and, more importantly, what's not selling to allocate funds properly for inventory purchasing.

Your store fixtures can usually be bought by scouring the classified pages in the local newspaper for bankruptcy auctions, sales by firms going out of business and opportunities to save money when a company upgrades its furniture. You can easily spend a small fortune when buying new display cases, cabinets, bookcases, desks and chairs. Buying used furniture, you will save money you can invest in your stamp inventory. Besides the newspaper, consult your phone directory for used furniture dealers and rental firms. Rental agencies often sell overstocked or discontinued pieces at significant savings.

Fluorescent lights remain the most cost-efficient way to light your general customer area. You can have incandescent or halogen lights at your counter for detailed stamp viewing. If you choose incandescent, use clamp-on swivel-arm lamps that you can take with you when you take tables at bourses.

One or two Tarifold display stands will be just what you need to display popular sets and promotional material on your counter and then at bourses.

Be sure to have plenty of APS membership applications by your check-out area. Other handouts could include mount charts and price lists, as well as philatelic supply price lists. Consider rubber-stamping them with your discount policy.

Provide tongs for your clientele to use in the store and at shows. Also have some extra black trays and watermark fluid handy for customers to check stamps. Be comfortable when customers double check. If you have done your job right, you will be right. Every time customers verify your statements, their confidence in you soars. On the few occasions you're wrong, you want to know that, too. Your readiness to acknowledge your humanity quickly and gracefully also will show customers you are reliable and honest.

The bourse dealer has a few extra essentials. I display my unusual wares under a clear piece of plastic that is anchored by two-inch clear weather-stripping tape to eliminate theft. The panel is anchored to my table cover.

Notice I said "my" table cover. Do not settle for the bed sheet or cheap plastic or paper covers provided with the table rental. A nice piece of cloth will make your table stand out from the others.

Visit your local fabric store and get something attractive and subdued. Two such covers that I use with much success are a deep green vinyl and a blue and off-white plaid in a polyester and cotton blend. I alternate their use from show to show so that I create the appearance of change. After every show, clean or launder your table cover.

Carry two of your clamp-on swivel-arm lamps for each 8-foot table you rent. Set them in about 2 feet from each table end. Veteran dealers carry spare bulbs as well.

Prospective clients must know who you are. Either invest in a professional sign or choose an alternative like a "message sign," on which you can set up the letters. (Grayarc's M686 was perfect for my needs when I bought one years ago. The set consisted of two separate pieces with white backgrounds and 630 tabbed characters, including attention-getting red.)

Other essentials include inexpensive tongs for customer use, glassines (rubber stamped with your name, address, phone number and slogan) into which you'll place your customer's purchases, several sharpened pencils, a supply of your latest price list or mail auction catalog, business cards and give-aways like ball point pens imprinted with your data. Other helpful items are note paper (I use 5½ x8½-inch) with your name, address and slogan imprinted. The paper doubles as customer receipt and quote forms. Remember also to take your calculator with print-out tape and extra batteries and a cash box with plenty of change and $1 bills.

How does one transport all of this material, plus the required stock, to shows? I use a couple of footlockers that are just the right height for the stockbook binders to stand upright. The lockers also are wide enough so that in one of them I can put my two file drawers of glassines and other items. The lamps, books and stationery items are carried in a heavy cardboard carton. Everything fits nicely in my hatchback. When I arrive at my destination, I take everything in on my heavy-duty hand truck.

There are times when you will go out on an evaluation or appraisal. The type of catalogs and reference books you take will depend on the type of material you are called on to inspect.

Primarily, the basic list includes:
• Showgard #607 clear perforation gauge.
• Showgard #902 professional stamp tongs.

- Black glass watermark dish.
- Watermark fluid.
- 4x and 10x magnifiers.
- Ultraviolet light - short and long wave.
- Legal pads, pens and pencils.
- Calculator with print-out tape and extra batteries.
- Standard release or contract.
- Your checkbook.

Having the right tools and equipment makes anyone's job easier. This is especially true for stamp dealers.

Chapter 8
The Professional Approach

Because effective communications are vital to the success of any business, it is important for stamp dealers to speak and write professionally.

A good place to start is with first contacts. The collector who calls or comes to your store may categorize you, to your lasting benefit or detriment, based on the first impression you create. Because most stamp dealerships are one-person operations, the important first contact usually is with *YOU*.

Courtesy goes beyond niceness and politeness. It begins with the first spoken word and the tone in which it is delivered. What would you rather hear on the other end of the telephone? A bright, cheerful "Good morning. XYZ Stamp Company. How may I help you?" or, a dismal, almost hostile, "Hul-lo"? Condition yourself to be bright and accommodating if you want to stay in business.

(By the way, people wouldn't be calling or coming to your store if you couldn't help them. Asking, "How may I help you?" starts the conversation with more clarity and focus than asking, "May I help you?")

If you are working out of your home through a post office box, consider getting a second telephone number and using it strictly for your stamp business. You can have it listed in the directory without an address, and you won't have to tell friends and neighbors you are in the stamp business unless you want them to know.

If you get a two-line phone for your desk, you'll also be able to make outgoing calls on the household line while keeping the incoming stamp line free. Also, get the call-waiting service. Busy signals bother customers who are ready to buy and want to do it now.

Telephone courtesy is more than just the greeting, order taking and thank you. Sometimes, a special item comes in for a customer, and you want to do the customer the courtesy of letting him or her know you've located the long-sought treasure. Before calling, make a cheat sheet. Any piece of paper will do. Write the phone number and the first and last names of the collector and spouse. If the spouse answers, he or she will be complimented and impressed to be greeted by name. Also jot down the specific information on the item that you are calling about and your firm price. Anything you can use to advantage belongs on your cheat sheet. If you are able to offer this piece at $50 less than a similar piece just bought at a New York auction, by all means mention it.

Make a note of the time and be sure to allow for time zones. Don't call anyone during the dinner hour or too late at night. I have found that the best calling times are between 7 p.m. and 9 p.m. at the collector's end.

You'll also have to deal with complaint calls, justified or otherwise. In general, it's best to let the caller get the complaint all out. Until the caller has told you what's on his or her mind and believes you have understood what was said, problem solving won't work.

When a person calls to complain, automatically shift yourself into neutral and put your feelings aside for a while. Remember that your goal is to respect the other person's view, even if it is different from yours, and to keep the customer's business or even to increase it. Start by saying things like, "Tell me about your problem" and "I'd like to know more about that." Responses like "I see" and "Uh huh" begin to let the customer know you are hearing.

Also, say back to the customer what he or she is saying to you. It's a way of being sure you're getting the real message and of letting the customer know at the same time you are understanding. It might go like this: "I understand. You're saying you're really frustrated because your order arrived a week late, even though you know it's the post office's fault." The collector will say something like, "That's right!" or "No, you don't understand. I'm mad because you cashed my check three weeks before you shipped my order."

When you've let the customer vent and you're sure you really do understand, you can ask something like, "What would work best for you now?" or "How can we solve this so you and I both are winners?" The idea is to get the customer working with you as a team to insure he or she is satisfied in a way that is fair to everyone involved.

If you start making excuses, attacking the customer in return or getting emotional, someone will win and someone will lose, rather than everyone winning. No matter how it ends up, you are the real loser if a customer goes elsewhere because your pride or your lack of human relations skill got in the way.

Sometimes, a customer just wants a shoulder to cry on because of a personal misfortune. The call may begin with some outlandish request like asking if you have any first-day covers of Scott No. 1 in stock. Then the collector may begin sharing woes. Again, the tell-me-more approach helps people feel better and be satisfied with their contacts with you. If there's been an event like a death in the family, you can say things like "I can tell you really miss your mom" or "You really seem blue now."

Emphasize listening. People with major problems don't want you to fix things. That implies they are incapable of handling their own lives. People under stress want a caring human to talk to. Very little response is necessary from you. Particularly avoid saying that you know just how the caller is feeling (you can't possibly, although you might guess) or that everything will be all right (it may not be).

If you don't have time or patience for such exchanges, consider becoming a wholesale dealer who has minimum public contact. You'll be doing yourself and collectors a favor. The dealer who comes off as disinterested or rude will soon have plenty of time on his or her hands. Collectors will flock elsewhere or will dip into the mail-order waters.

The same principles of cheerfulness and being a good listener apply to face-to-face contacts at your store or show table. A friendly "Hello! How are you?" will go much further than a nod or a grunt.

The customer is dealing with you because he or she has genuine interest in stamp collecting. It is a person who literally is saying, "Here I am. I'm a stamp collector, and I came to share my enthusiasm and to buy for my collection."

Your part of the transaction is to show genuine caring and willingness to serve. The key word is "genuine." Give your clients credit for above-average intelligence. They spot phonies at 100 paces. Be genuine and enthusiastic or go into some other line of work.

A collector may very well be checking you out the first time he or she visits. Your stock, as well as your personality, are being evaluated. Be relaxed and cordial. Establish a dialogue. Always project professionalism. Be friendly, courteous and—above all else—be patient. Perhaps nothing will be bought today. However, mental notes are being taken for the future. Encourage another visit. Attempt to get the collector on your mailing list. Invite a want list. Above all else, avoid being pushy and coming off as a hard-sell specialist. Tread slowly at first and be rewarded later with steady patronage.

Be equally polite, helpful and courteous to children. Don't scorn them like so many irascible dealers do who can't see the forest for the trees. Sure they are inquisitive and want to touch everything. They're kids! Weren't you one once?

While helping a dealer at his booth at an ASDA show a few years ago, I heard the unpleasant, "Oh no! Here come the kids" as a busload of school children were about to enter the hall. The sound was echoed by several others. I chastised the offensive dealers!

Today's young collectors are the future's Luff Award winners. Without new blood going to the heart of philately, the hobby will stagnate and eventually die. As dealers, we have a vested interest in the futures of our hobby and our livelihoods. We must encourage the youngsters. Treat them with all the dignity and respect that you would an adult and think of yourself as a Johnny Appleseed sowing orchards for the hobby.

Give sound advice to all of your customers when they seek help. Be well versed in all areas of philately and be ready to share your wisdom. You'll be asked how to collect, what to collect, how to exhibit and numerous other questions.

And don't scorn topical collecting either. I once had a youngster come in my shop asking for whales on stamps. I had a decent British stock on hand and was able to show, and sell, several nice sets. I further promised that if he would return next Saturday morning I would have more to show him. Next Saturday found my new friend in the company of his father. I let the youth examine the sets and then I pulled out some covers. All were from sound stamp-issuing nations.

As the son eagerly examined his new found treasures, his father called me aside to tell me how much he appreciated my taking the time with his son and that I was the first dealer they had met who treated his son with respect. The son snapped up everything that was shown him and asked about a set of tongs. I gave him a rounded-end style that I felt would be suitable for his young hands and didn't even think of charging him anything for the tongs.

The following Saturday found my two new friends visiting me once again. This time Dad brought his U.S. album and filled in quite a few early spaces. There is a moral here. I'm glad you grasped it.

You will do well to understand early that your customers are your most valuable assets. Always roll out the red carpet. Treat customers like royalty, and you'll be rewarded royally. A facial expression often says more than words. You already may know that social scientists have found first impressions are formed 55 percent on the basis of your body language (including facial expressions), 35 percent on your tone of voice and 7 percent on the words you say.

Never scowl or show frustration with your customers. It's not an easy business to be sure. Any service business has its share of moaners and groaners. However, the way you handle them will determine your success. And, in the process of acting caring and cheerful, you'll probably feel better about yourself and really be that way more of the time.

How you handle your mail is just as important as your personal contacts. The pen really is mightier than the sword, and it's just as easy to smile on paper as it is in person.

One never knows what the daily mail will bring. Hope springs eternal for a never ending flow of nice orders. Then again, anything and everything turns to quicksand some days.

There is no right or wrong way to open your mail. Just find a system you are comfortable with. I prefer to organize mine into four piles in desktop letter trays that are stacked top to bottom, one through four.

Orders are stacked in the first, and hopefully tallest, pile. They are shipped the same day I receive them whenever possible. Envelopes are stapled to the backs of actual orders and payments are paper-clipped on top. Why do I keep envelopes? If I receive multiple orders for an item that I only have one of, I give it to the earliest postmark. I believe in playing fair. You also might be amazed at the many order forms that arrive without the names and addresses of the senders, even though there's ample space on the forms.

My next pile contains inquiries that need an immediate reply. They include want lists, requests for price lists and replies to earlier correspondence from me.

Pile three is for correspondence that can wait a day or two to be answered. Perhaps it is a request for a price on some item I don't stock. I'll have to make a call or two to get my cost and availability. Rather than make these calls in shotgun fashion, I prefer to do them about twice a week. This helps to reduce my phone bill because I can inquire about several items during one call. It also saves me quite a bit of time, which means money.

Another type of letter that sits on pile three is the one, with a self-addressed, stamped envelope, that asks for information that can only be obtained by consulting my reference library. There are days when these inquiries will be replied to in the afternoon mail. However, orders and want lists always come first.

The final pile is the most interesting. Whenever you hear me refer to my "four pile," you'll know why. These are the shameless requests for time-consuming research, or information, that arrive without the courtesy of an SASE. There was a time when I answered everything. My "four pile" was significantly smaller then.

A word of caution. As you prosper as a dealer, you can expect your own "four pile" to increase similarly. At the beginning, I strongly recommend you answer every piece of mail. You never know who is testing you.

I send a personal note with each order concisely and politely thanking the customer. A new order form and whatever stuffers I'm using at the current time also are included. I handle requests for price lists the same way. Stuffers and a short, friendly "Thank you for taking the time to answer our ad in the philatelic press" accompany each reply.

Some want lists may require you to make a call, especially if a scarce, not-easily-replaced item is involved. Sometimes a call can help you turn a small account into a big one. A note from your customer about a promotion at work or an inheritance are the kinds of clues you'll receive that the customer may be in a position to indulge himself or herself more.

Avoid pre-judging your mail once it is opened. You really can't tell who the big spenders will be. Many inexperienced dealers make the mistake of figuring doctors and lawyers, or persons they know to be wealthy, to be automatic big accounts. Just because someone requests your lists does not mean that orders will be forthcoming. Some of my best customers began as routine postal-card inquiries, contrary to conventional dealer wisdom that says requests without SASE's are poor prospects. Remember, if you are offering free information, it makes sense for your prospective customer to save on postage.

Another type of inquiry that does not need an SASE is the want list, especially if you advertise that you actively seek them. I know of some dealers who will not bother to reply to want lists from "strangers" without SASEs. I answer virtually all such letters. An exception is the mimeographed list containing dozens of items. These missives obviously are being sent to equally large numbers of dealers with the hope of saving a small amount of money by going with the lowest bidder. You can do without this type of collector.

If you "circular file" any other requests, you are throwing away the potential for future business as well.

Speaking of want lists, if you are going to handle them, you had better learn to define them. To quote Kenneth A. Wood in *This is Philately,* "A want list is a listing, usually by catalog number, of stamps that a collector requires for his collection." There is no doubt this is the best, most concise definition of want list I have ever seen. Please note the key word "requires."

Most collectors would like to substitute "needs" for "requires." Many of them think of a want list as a glorified "wish list." Very few consider it a request to purchase stamps. Thus, it becomes your job to educate your customers about what want lists are and the obligations that go with sending them to you.

I advise my customers that a want list sent to me is considered a firm order to purchase the stamps in the condition described and at a competitive price within 30 days of the date of the postmark. I further tell them that if a price quote is what they want, they should request a quotation and provide an SASE. I waive the envelope when I'm dealing with a regular customer.

My obligation is to make every attempt to purchase want-list items for my customer and to fill the list within the 30 days. I will price competitively and honor my return policy if the stamps fail to meet the customer's approval. Usually, I will have most of the items in stock anyway; so there is little expense procuring them. A knowledgeable collector won't hesitate to deal with you on this basis if he or she knows you give a fair deal.

Servicing want lists is a profitable operation. Too much trouble? Only if you are adverse to making money.

The stamp business itself is a profitable operation. Why do some fail at it? Because they don't run it like a business. The stamp business is, in many ways, unlike any other. However, dealers also can be effective business people. It takes dedication to the task at hand, plenty of study, logic and common sense.

If you receive a nice order with a personal check as full payment from a new customer who furnishes an APS membership number as a reference, what do you do? I contact the American Philatelic Society and check the member's standing, explaining the purpose of my call. If I get a good report, I ship the order immediately. An APS member is not likely to jeopardize his or her good philatelic name and risk expulsion by tendering a bad check.

For other orders received with checks, use common sense. A customer who has already ordered twice before for a total of $60 is very unlikely to stick you for $25. Ship the order.

The best way to be clear about check terms is to print them in your conditions of sale. Most dealers stipulate that orders are held until checks clear. Checks take no longer than five banking days from deposit to clear, regardless of what your bank may tell you. Chances are that they will clear in two or three days. To be on the safe side, wait the five banking days, contact your bank, and if all is OK, ship the order.

Credit can be a touchy subject. You'll be granting terms eventually to your better accounts. My terms are net 30 days. When a customer is late paying, what do you do? By law, all customers get a 15-day grace period before you can notify them they are in arrears. On the 45th day from date of invoice, I send a gentle reminder. Sometimes an invoice is forgotten though oversight or some extenuating circumstance. Most of the time it is unpaid because of a "cash flow" problem. The collector overextended and needs a little more time.

This is where the situation could be handled easily if the customer lets you know what was happening. Often the collector is silent because of embarrassment. When sending the first reminder, be sure to mention that a partial payment can be sent now with the balance within two weeks. Offer to put the amount on a credit card. Do what you can to make it easy for the customer.

If you don't receive a reply within two weeks of mailing the reminder, send a second notice. This time I suggest slightly stronger language. I remind the account that it has now been 60 days from the date of the original invoice, which makes the account 30 days past due. I suggest that immediate contact be made to discuss the situation. If another two weeks pass without payment, I send a final notice or make a call. I tell the person I will need to turn the debt over for collection if it isn't paid at once. So far, I haven't had to follow through because my final notices or calls always have produced a check.

Should you use a collection agency? Absolutely, if you have to. It is good business practice to pursue your debts. The service of two collection agencies, at a discounted rate, is just one of the benefits of ASDA membership.

What happens to the customers that you've sent the three notices to, or turned over for collection? Will they ever buy from you again? Probably not. And they probably are the kinds of customers you can live without.

Delinquent account services advertise in *The Stamp Wholesaler*. Avail yourself of the services of these firms. They distribute lists of collectors who have had credit and payment problems with other dealers, and their fees are surprisingly small.

Another opportunity to make money is doing appraisals. Sooner or later, every dealer is asked to do them. Appraisals serve many purposes. Gift, probate, sale, insurance and capital gains tax are the five most popular varieties. Gift and probate appraisals are identical, except that gift appraisals establish the value of a philatelic gift made by a living person and probate appraisals determine the value of a philatelic bequest by a deceased person. Use replacement costs when establishing the value in these two instances.

A sale appraisal is performed for someone who has a collection for sale. Usually, it is someone who has inherited material and has no idea of the fair market value. It would be easier to make a cash offer if the material is the kind you ordinarily stock. If not, offer an appraisal based on current buy prices.

The insurance appraisal is often called for when coverage is applied for or an increase is desired. Actually, you can perform these routinely for your client every year as values do change. Here again, use replacement value as the basis.

Appraisals for capital gains tax are supplied on an estimated cost basis from the owner's receipts alone.

The American Society of Appraisers recommends that, for all appraisals, a flat fee or an hourly rate be charged. Some stamp dealers instead base fees on a percentage of appraised value, which can make it look like they have inflated the value to earn a larger fee.

Be sure to qualify your customer as the legal owner of the stated material. Have the owner stipulate to you the type of appraisal that is sought, and be clear that your fee is net, payable upon the presentation of invoice.

Your appraisal form itself should be drawn up by your attorney. The most important part of it is the disclaimer. Mine is a bit wordy: "The foregoing appraisal is made with the understanding that the appraiser assumes no liability with respect to any action that may be taken on the basis of this appraisal. Furthermore, all statements regarding condition, gum, quality and authenticity are made to the best of our knowledge without removal from mountings, holders or albums and without tests or expertization, unless so stated above. In accepting this appraisal, the owner agrees to the preceding in its entirety."

Chapter 9
Your Mailing List

Your most valuable asset is not your magnificent stock of early U.S. stamps and covers. It is your customer list. During a career, the average stamp dealer spends more money on advertising than his or her final inventory brings when sold. Most of the ad dollars are spent just to bring clients into the fold.

Dealers zealously guard their lists, and the smart ones tend their lists like farmers. They sow seeds to acquire more names, weed out names that no longer produce and plan for large harvests. Everything is focused on making your customer list yield maximum profits.

There are only a few ways to get new names. Advertising brings in most of them. I already mentioned that classified advertising sections of philatelic newspapers are low-cost, effective places to find new customers. Successful, established dealers know new customers constantly are needed to replace those lost through attrition.

Renting names is another excellent way to add new clients that often is overlooked by dealers. Publications like *The Stamp Wholesaler* and *Stamp Collector* newspapers rent subscriber and other names for mailing to one time only. Typical costs are $80 per thousand names, with a minimum of 5,000 names per rental. In the mail-list rental industry, if you want to mail to the list a second time, you need to rent it again.

(Companies know how many times you mail to their lists because they insert decoy names and addresses in the lists they rent to you. Each time a piece is mailed to a decoy, the person at the decoy address returns the piece to the company that rented the list to you.)

Legally, the names remain the property of the company that rents them to you until a customer responds to your offer from the rented list. The customer's name and address then become your property and can be added to your list.

That provides you with a way around renting lists a second time. Pack a coupon and a business reply envelope (or postage-paid postal

card) in your mailing and strongly invite the collector to request being placed on your mailing list. Paying the postage for the collector
makes it easy to respond to you. Also hook him or her with some
inducement like "10 percent (or more, if you wish) new-customer discount from our soon-to-be-released comprehensive United States price
list." The idea is to get the collector to take the initiative and ask you
to place him or her on your mailing list.

If you want more information about the *Stamp Collector/Stamp
Wholesaler* mailing lists, contact the newspapers' mail list manager,
Aggressive List Management, 18-2 East Dundee Road, Suite 101,
Barrington, IL 60010, or phone 708-304-4030, FAX 708-304-4032.

The American Philatelic Society also makes member names available to its dealer members. Check with it for complete details. One
advantage to APS names is that you can obtain fewer than 5,000 at a
time. The APS, like the stamp newspapers, will screen you to ensure
that your company and/or product meets its standards and that your
intentions are legitimate. It must, above all else, protect its members'
best interests and safeguard against possible theft.

You can also purchase names from firms that advertise under the
"Mailing Lists" category in the classified pages. The going rate is $25
per 1,000 names with trial quantities of 100 names usually available
for $4 or $5. When you buy (rather than rent) names, they are yours to
make repeated mailings to.

The type of individual that you attract here differs quite a bit from
the ones you'll obtain from the rental sources that we mentioned. The
2.5-cent name you purchase can be a collector who, unbeknownst to
the seller, recently gave up the hobby. Or perhaps the collector is a
small buyer of approvals composed of canceled-to-order worldwide
short sets. You also could find treasure hunters, or the people who do
nothing else than request free price lists and other information from
stamp dealers. Sometimes the list will contain stamp show attendees,
who may be poor mail-order buyers. You might even get some bona
fide good buyers.

It's all part of renting and buying mailing lists. List owners cannot
possibly know the current collecting habits of all the names in their
files. They only know the people on their lists have expressed some
kind of stamp interest. And that is exactly what you get, a list of potential customers, many of whom won't end up buying from you and
some of whom will.

You can increase the odds in your favor by using lists of more highly
selected collectors from places like the hobby newspapers. To find a

publication like *Stamp Collector,* the individual had to go to some
trouble because stamp collecting publications are not found on many
newsstands. *SC* subscribers also qualify as serious collectors because
one does not spend money on a stamp paper and read it week after
week unless one is a collector.

The APS list is one of the best. Its 58,000 names reflect the cream
of the hobby — serious collectors to be sure. Many are highly specialized, and this can be a drawback for new dealers. The APS
member's needs might exceed the capabilities of the rookie's stock.
Many APS members also have obtained all but the difficult-to-find
stamps they want after years of collecting.

The best list you can get is one from a dealer who is either going out
of business or changing his or her product line or approach. A classic
example would be the dealer who, up until now, had been handling
U.S., British Commonwealth and Western Europe. She now decides
to go exclusively with the United States and offers her mailing lists of
the British and European areas separately. The British area dealer who
purchases that list gets active, interested buyers, rather than prospects.

Another way to acquire names is to copy the "New Members" section of the specialty society journals that include addresses. Here's a
tip. Wait four weeks after you receive the publication before you do
your mailing. Most dealers send their literature at once. The new
member's mailbox can be flooded with philatelic material at first.
There is a better than average chance your offering will be caught in
the shuffle and will be thrown away. Without competition, you stand
the best chance of having your pitch read and acted on.

And, of course, when you advertise a listing of sets for sale in a
stamp publication, you surely will add to your mailing list the names
of all who order.

So there you have the five primary ways of adding names and building your mailing list: (1) Advertising; (2) Rentals who request being
added to your list; (3) Purchasing names; (4) New members of philatelic societies; and (5) Customers who purchase from your list-pros-
pecting ads.

Now that you have the names, what do you do with them? You develop and maintain a basic prospect file and mailing list system.

Seasoned dealers who routinely mail to several thousand collectors
at a time will have their mailing lists and other business matters on
computer. For newer dealers, I suggest a system I developed for myself during years of trial and error.

My first step in handling an inquiry or order is to make an entry on a ruled, 3x5-inch index card. If the reply is from a collector who previously was unknown to me, I record "vital stats," on the card. (If the collector is already on file, the customer card is pulled and the appropriate information is added.)

I use six vital statistics:

Name and Address — I enter the last name first for ease in alphabetizing. I ignore titles like Mr., Ms. and Dr. unless the collector "signs" with them.

Phone Number — This is the most useful information on the card. Whenever I receive an order or want list, I try to get a phone number through telephone information. For an especially large order from a new client, calling the client is an excellent way to verify an address and is handy if the collector is not a member of a philatelic society.

Want-list Code Number — For example, "B2" tells me the customer has submitted a want list of fine-to-very fine, unused stamps of the period from the Pan-American issue through Scott 701. If it were "b2," the lower case "b" would inform me that used stamps were desired. The grade and time frame remain the same. I also enter the information when a collector tells me his or her collecting goal in a letter.

Collecting Interests —Your key to bigger profits. Find out what your customer collects. This is different from the want-list or collecting goal mentioned above. This is an all-inclusive overview of his or her albums and stockbooks.

For example, the collector may submit a want list reflecting that he is primarily interested in filling some gaps in his album of the 1900 to 1940 period and in unused, fine-to-very fine condition.

On further inquiry I might learn that Mr. Doe collects a broad spectrum of U.S. singles and chooses used for the classic material. He also has a sideline collection of Special Delivery covers, as well as a pet topical collection, trains on stamps. Any and all such information will eventually reward me with larger sales.

Now I have an outlet for nice Special Delivery covers that come my way. I also am likely to find a couple of nice train stamp or R.P.O. cover lots in an auction catalog. While I, or my agent, examine the lots for my day-to-day operation, the train lots and Special Delivery covers also will be looked at. I'll report to my customer to see if there's any interest; there usually is.

If you don't acquire this valuable data, you might be left out in the cold while your competitors are going to the bank. You may want to encourage your customers to answer a few brief questions at the bottom of your order blank.

Society Memberships — Memberships, especially those of ASDA or APS members, can be a barometer of credit worthiness. New members of philatelic societies are prone to list their membership numbers on their correspondence. Veteran collectors like to show off a low number. However, those in-between members don't list their affiliations very often. Do yourself a favor. On the order blank, below the provision for name and address, leave a line that can be entitled "Society Memberships."

Customer History —This can tell me that on Aug. 15, 1990, Mr. Doe requested a price list of pre-1940 U.S. stamps that I had advertised in *Stamp Collector.* When the request came in, I knew the source from the "key" in my address. The next listing might tell me that on Sept. 7, an order arrived from this collector for several more items that I made a note of. If it were an order for multiple stamps, I might enter it as "Several F-VF, NH sets/singles 599-701, $63.50" to save space.

If the order had come from one of my listing ads, I would have coded it as L-SC to show that it came from a listing ad in *Stamp Collector.*

A "PC" notation tells me that payment was made by personal check. I didn't hesitate to send the order out at once because a quick glance at my card on Mr. Doe told me that he is a member of two prominent societies. If I had to hold the order for check clearance, due to lack of society membership, I would have made another entry on the card - "9-14-90 shipped 9-7 order. PC clear."

In addition, if Mr. Doe has purchased the Huguenot-Walloon and Lexington-Concord issues, I know his collection is not too advanced. If he is working backwards, as so many do, the next purchase might be the Pilgrim issue, 1922-25 definitives or perhaps the 1923-29 Rotary singles and coils. You can bet that if I have some nice stock of these items, I'll mention it in my thank-you letter. And now that I know Mr. Doe's collecting interests, I could mail him a special offers list of early U.S. used. My possibilities for continued profit are enormous.

Hopefully, Mr. Doe and I will do enough business to fill both sides of the index card. If we do, I'll mark the completed card in red ink with a numeral 1 at the top center and staple it behind a new card that will again contain all the vital stats.

Auxiliary information I always enter, in parenthesis after the phone number, is the first name of the spouse. You are almost certain to find this tidbit on the check. When I call for some reason and spouses answer, the personal touch is appreciated. They are impressed that I knew their names. At the end of the year, when Season's Greetings are being bestowed, you can personalize your message, which also is appreciated.

Because I produce many segmented mailings a year, I use colored cards in my customer file. Red indicates dealers. Green are No. 1 collectors. They are the steady customers who spent $100 or more during the past six months. Whenever someone reaches this glorified height, I pull his or her regular white card and staple the green one to it, being careful to record vital statistics again.

You may decide, as I do, to send frequent customers a periodic list of special offers as a reward for continued patronage. There also will be times when you want to send a wholesale list to your colleagues. Other dealers could turn out to be some of your best customers.

Keep your mailing list growing steadily by continually advertising for new prospects. Avoid complacency and falsely thinking you have enough names. You never can have enough.

Collectors constantly leave the hobby, temporarily or permanently. You have to fill the void. Collecting interests change, and your product line may no longer be suitable. Other collectors find new dealers and drop you unexpectedly.

Look for new names wherever and whenever possible. One technique I use is the buddy system. The reverse side of my order form is intentionally left blank. I ask my customers to use it for any comments they care to make. Besides writing want lists, requests for quotation, new collecting interests or personal notes, they know to use it for referrals.

The buddy system helps my customers as well as me. For every collector a customer recommends who spends $20 or more on stamps or supplies over time, I send my customer a $2 credit coupon.

Record keeping is easy. Yet another entry on the index card for this new prospect would be marked as follows; 8-22-93 Referred by John Doe. Pre-1940 PL sent. When the $20 purchase has been reached, John Doe receives his $2 credit, a thank-you note and a suggestion that he send more names.

Another aspect of getting the most from your mailing list is updating it periodically. Many dealers waste large sums on printing and postage to mail to so-called collectors who actually are "blowhards." You'll hear, "I'm going to buy those Zepps next," or "Keep sending me your lists even though I won't be able to buy anything for some time. I just finished off my collection of German States and I'm a little short of cash."

I keep my mailing list separated into four levels of activity, from "very much alive" to "dead."

Category 1: Customers who order on a regular basis and who have spent over $100 during the past six months.

Category 2: Those who have ordered at least once during the past year. You might see several small sales, adding up to maybe $40 or $50. You might have one sale for $75 or so about 10 months ago. These collectors need follow-ups.

Category 3: Requested a price list within the past year but haven't ordered yet. Also need follow-ups. Usually six months after the list was requested.

Category 4: Requested a price list more than a year ago but have not ordered. These collectors need a mortician.

What you need is to think about the message for you from this group. Are your prices too high? Is your stock too limited? Not enough extra-fine stamps to appeal to discriminating customers?

Following up customer inquiries and orders often results in new sales you otherwise might have lost, and feedback you definitely would not have received.

There is no set formula for when the first follow-up is most productive. It's a matter of your preference. One thing is certain. Not one, but two or more follow-ups are necessary to bring lost sheep back to the flock.

Avoid the trite approach that goes, "We haven't heard from you in some time, and if you do not order from this list we must remove your name from our mailing list." This message tells the customer you are anxious to drop him, whether it be now or in a couple of months.

Worse yet are dealers who send such notes after only two price lists have been sent. Prospects need time to study your offerings and to order. Collectors who request your list have shown some degree of interest. Give them the benefit of the doubt and allow six months for them to order. This will be three to six lists, depending on how frequently you mail. If they haven't ordered after six months, follow up then, and then two months later.

Briefly, my follow-up says I have a compelling desire to serve the collector's needs and to provide exactly the type of material he or she wants. I then ask my prospect if my stamps are the kind he seeks. If not, I ask what the collector would like to see offered. If funds are lacking, does the collector know about my lay-away plan and that I gladly accept Visa and MasterCard?

All this is topped off with a self-addressed, stamped envelope for good measure. This goodwill gesture assures a high response rate. The letter and SASE tells my customer he or she is very important to me and leaves the unspoken idea that a reply is expected. To my deep satisfaction, the system works well.

There may be dozens of reasons a prospect hasn't ordered quickly. For most collectors, family needs come first. Collecting is just a hobby.

If the first follow-up is not answered, I wait another two months. If no order still is forthcoming, I send a friendly postcard. It might say to be on the lookout for the new list I'm preparing to mail. I might even be bold enough to say that a special offers list was just mailed out to every customer who ordered at least once from my lists during the past six months. Does the collector wish to see a copy and take advantage of the sale as an inducement to order from the regular list? Every situation is different, and I mostly play it by ear.

Follow-ups to my "deceased" file (Category 4) are made only if I have some price lists left over from a recent mailing. I select a few hundred names, include a discount coupon valid for 60 days and advise the prospect that this is a last-ditch effort to land his or her business. I select at least 200 names because I save quite a lot by using bulk-rate mail and need to meet the minimum number of pieces.

If there is no response to all of this effort on my part, the collector is declared officially dead and removed from my files.

You also can use follow-ups effectively when sending out an order. Earlier we mentioned the letter that went to Mr. Doe along with his order. This went out in anticipation of his ordering from among several sets in the near future. It is a type of follow-up.

Another is asking if the collector's want list is up to date. Ask if there have been any changes in collecting interests. You can offer some newly acquired gem that you're sure would fit in just right with the rest of his or her collection.

Every time that you place your name and product line in front of a customer, you are opening the door to potential business. Follow-ups are an important ingredient in a recipe for success. Your profits will taste much better when you learn to use follow-ups effectively.

Chapter 10
The Grand Opening

There's nothing quite like it! The anticipation has your adrenaline flowing. As the big day draws near, your nerves become jangled. Butterflies float in your stomach. Relax! It all goes with your Grand Opening.

If you are opening a store, the feelings can be even more intense than those of a new bourse or mail-order dealer. In a store, the overhead is greater; so the sales and profits must be, too.

We discussed in Chapter 3 the pros and cons of the various ways of dealing. Regardless of the avenue you choose to travel, however, you must announce your destination. You need to advertise to the philatelic community who you are, where you are located and what hours you'll keep as we discussed in Chapter 4. Too many new store owners depend on their storefront to bring them a meager customer base. You need a healthy customer base to make a good living from stamps.

Trumpet your opening in every way imaginable. Start with the stamp sections of as many Sunday newspapers as are circulated in your area. If there are no stamp sections, look for the closest match available. Leisure sections, book sections and entertainment sections are possibilities. You need more newspapers than the one you favor. You can't assume all stamp collectors share your opinions.

Also get yourself in the pages of surrounding communities — especially so if there is a metropolis within 50 miles of your location. When I opened my store (about 20 miles north of downtown Philadelphia) I not only bought space in the local papers, but I went to the *Philadelphia Inquirer* as well.

The sprawling city of Trenton, N.J., was not ignored either. It was about 10 miles east of my store. The *Trenton Times* did not fail me. It delivered some very important customers, some of whom are still with me years later.

Yes, the expense was tremendous as I added up all the invoices. Do you know what? The profits were worth it!

Telephone book yellow pages are essential for any dealer who wants to do business locally. Be sure to give your exact location and store hours. State exactly what it is that you buy and sell. If you are located near some landmark, mention it. For example, "Just half a mile east of the Public Service bus terminal."

Paid advertising is just one way to distribute your message. Press releases also can be effective, and they're free. Contact the business editor of every newspaper that is distributed within 100 miles of your store. Supply an announcement of your grand opening for the financial section and offer to supply information for an article about you and your business, too. Editors look for reader interest, and you'll have to do a good selling job by telling the editor why the article will be more interesting to readers than other news that may be competing for the same space. The more human interest, the more likely the editor is to want the article.

Mention how the CIA Inverts sparked a rejuvenation of one of the world's oldest and most pursued hobbies. Think of a few other slants and talk them up. Don't be too pushy or too wordy. Prepare a little script ahead of time. A couple of short paragraphs taking a minute or less to read is sufficient. Your job is merely to whet the editor's thirst for more. If you can accomplish that, you will most certainly get yourself into print.

After you've thoroughly covered your local publications, send news releases to editors of every major philatelic publication and to the stamp editor of the local newspapers. News releases are covered in greater detail in Chapter 5. Be sure to use this magnificent form of free advertising.

Radio also can be effective. When I became a dealer, I invited myself onto a local call-in radio show. It gave me a half hour of not only answering questions from the listening audience but, more importantly, announced my store address, phone number and hours. It brought in a flock of customers. I take every opportunity to be on a show.

If a renowned philatelist lives nearby, consider inviting him or her to your store for the grand opening celebration. Highlight the information in your publicity campaign.

And knock on the manager's door at every post office you can find. Introduce yourself by mentioning your new store, and be sure to leave printed material with your location, phone number and hours. Ask if you can post a notice since many postal customers also will be interested. Handing a supply of your business cards to the window clerks can help, too. You might be pleasantly surprised at the number of people who inquire at their local post office about stamp dealers.

Strike up the band! The big day finally has arrived. You are now in the stamp business. You have great expectations. You envision wall-to-wall customers clamoring for your Zepps. However, the reality is that you have countless competitors for that almighty leisure dollar. You have to fight for your share.

If you've promoted your grand opening as outlined you will have a roomful of people for most of that glorious day, especially if you've advertised some opening-day specials. The trick is to encourage those inquiring souls to come back, again and again.

Comfortable chairs and good lighting are not enough. Provide watermark fluid and trays for anyone who wants to verify your assertions. It's natural for people to check, and it reinforces their trust in you when they find you're giving them accurate information. Also have good tongs and a supply of note paper and pencils handy. Make certain your name, address, phone number and hours are everywhere possible.

Providing all the comforts of home, reasonable prices, a cheery atmosphere and a friendly disposition will go a long way toward convincing the first-time shopper to make many more return visits — and soon.

Guard against allowing opening-day jitters to transform you into a hard-sell dealer. For the most part, collectors are just checking you out today. You'll see those smiling faces again if you make them feel welcome and relaxed.

If you're beginning as a bourse dealer, you'll want to herald your entry into the business, too. The same principles of advertising, news releases and customer comforts apply in your case.

The mail order dealer's opening is coincidental with the first published ad. The dealer also will want to advertise his or her business opening and to send news releases to the philatelic press. Personal reply notes to new customers will be the way he or she shows friendliness and invites repeat business.

Almost all new dealers share fear. They fear the uncertainty of their chosen profession and fear they may not make enough money to care for their families. Once you prove to yourself you can make it, you will see firsthand that there's no business like the stamp business. The exhilaration of opening those doors every morning and of waiting for the daily mail is unmatched anywhere else in the business world for me. The stamp profession is so varied and so unique. You never know just what's coming next.

It would be impossible for me to discuss every possible daily encounter. Instead, I'll introduce you to a few of the more common situations you're likely to face in time.

For instance, what do you do when collector after collector brings in endless quantities of recent sheets and plate blocks? Say "No thank you." If you don't learn to say no, you soon will find yourself low on cash and sitting on stamps with poor profit potential, not to mention that those lovely dollars could have been put to better use buying collections with high sales potential. Don't listen to your would-be sellers who say the stamps are always worth face value because you can always use them for postage. Simply tell the individual to do the same thing — take them home and use them for postage.

Early in my career, I bought quantities of plate blocks and sheets at or near face value just to balance out my stock. I didn't know any better, and I spent more than a year licking stamps that seemed like such a great buy at the time. For you, there's no excuse; you know now.

I never have figured out collectors (and I use the term loosely) who walk through our doors and ask, "Do you buy stamps?" I wonder where they think our stamps come from? Before you say yes, consider the possibility of consenting to buy every child's collection in town. A better response is, "We gladly purchase stamps we currently need for our stock."

You've qualified your terms, and you haven't ruffled any feathers in the process. A good policy is to purchase only the type of material you offer for sale. If you don't sell Disney sets, don't buy them. Refer the individual to the source from which they came. The same goes for everything else: modern first-day covers, plate blocks, et al.

You also will hear often: "Your prices are a bit too high! Can't you do any better?" I wonder if any of these otherwise timid souls would ask their shoe merchant for a better price. They wouldn't.

Stick to your guns. Price your stamps fairly. Grade them properly. Then relax. True collectors recognize accurately graded, competitively priced stamps and buy without hesitation if they need what you have. You can do without chiselers. The same people who would not think twice about paying a doctor or lawyer for advice seem to think that stamp dealers work solely out of passion. They seem to think that there is a hidden source of income that eliminates the need to turn a profit on a philatelic transaction.

In another situation you'll face, the reasoning always seems to be the same. "I just want to know what they're worth." Well, I offer appraisals, which require expertise and time, for a fee. The reply often is "I don't see why you are charging me. I'm giving you an opportunity to buy them." Fine, if I buy them, then the appraisal fee is waived. Meanwhile, I don't work for nothing, and neither do I suggest that you do.

"Do you sell by Scott, Harris or Brookman?" is frequently heard. Seems a reasonable enough question, doesn't it? Ask the prospect to visit the local supermarket. Seek out the store manager and ask how the store arrives at its prices. The collector will look at you in a puzzled and troubled manner. He or she probably will not see the significance of your remark.

The next question will be, "Tell me, at what percentage of your selling price do you buy?" Again, the same hearty soul should be told to ask the clothing merchant to reveal his profit structure to a stranger.

You can do little else but politely say that you are a merchant and that just like any other merchant your profits are personal.

And remember that most collectors are wonderful folks. You will make many friendships. The good experiences will far outweigh the bad. Once you learn how to respond comfortably and neutrally to the stinkers and your business becomes established, you will join the rest of us who would not do anything else for a living.

Prepare yourself for a typical day in the life of a stamp dealer, and you will remain positive while dealing with the challenges.

Chapter 11
Plan Ahead

Stamp dealing gives you the freedom you crave, satisfies your unending love affair with philately and provides the income you need. Now think about substituting the word "want" for the word "need" in the part about income. What a difference!

Virtually anyone with common sense, a decent stock of stamps and a good mailing list can make a living in our hobby. What separates successful dealers from those eking out an existence is good business sense. Many dealers haven't developed it because they are passionate about stamps, rather than doing business, and don't have formal business training.

An amazing number of dealers act as if the normal rules and principles of business don't apply to them. They don't take inventory, don't keep track of what they pay for stamps in their stock, don't advertise, keep the best stamps in their stock for their own collections and so forth. Then they wonder why they don't do well.

It's like taking someone who loves and knows photography and setting him or her up as proprietor of a professional studio. Our photographer has an array of lenses and knows how to use them. He is a student of lighting and carefully meters each shot. He has had his own darkroom for 10 years and can produce beautiful enlargements. He owns and uses an extensive photographic library and knows the latest techniques and trends.

You would almost bet that our friend would be a rousing success. Wrong! He doesn't know an emulsion sheet from a balance sheet. Trying to run a business without commercial skills is like trying to take pictures without film in the camera.

You must be a sharp businessperson to be a successful stamp dealer. And it is only success that will provide you with the income that you "want," rather than merely the income you "need" to eke out a living.

Unfortunately, there are no precise guidelines to guarantee your success. No formula is sure to make you rich.

Success only comes to those who work hard for it. You need the fortitude to get up one more time than you are knocked down—after being knocked down again and again. There are long hours, frustrating customers, losses caused by your inexperience or inattention. You begin to wonder if the light at the end of the tunnel is a train coming toward you.

Once you have absorbed and begun to practice the guidelines in this book, you will be well on your way. You will have avoided many of the pitfalls that trap the unwary.

However, there is that one gray area that only you can develop—business sense. You do it by creating a target and then by adjusting your aim every time you miss the bull's-eye. In other words, *you plan ahead.*

You develop a business plan, and then you exert the self-discipline to stick to it. For example, if you've set your sights on getting 30 new consignors this year for your mail-bid sales and just five have come aboard during the first three months, that's feedback that you need to adjust your aim. You still want those 30 new consignors, and you're two to three shy for the first quarter. You're going to have to try something else to get them.

Since your primary method of attracting new consignors is through advertising, make some working assumptions that your message isn't motivating potential consignors, your ad is too small to draw an adequate response or perhaps both problems exist.

Let's say the ad is large enough. Then, the answer must lie with the message, the ad's word structure.

If you are settling with consignors within 30 days of the sale date, be sure your ad highlights your quick payment. Because most houses pay in 45 to 60 days, this is a unique selling point and a reason for collectors to consign to you. Look for other important selling points and be sure they are mentioned prominently. Sell your business every way you can that is truthful.

Chances are that you'll attract more consignors. Are you getting enough to hit your target by year end? If you are, raise your sights as soon as your figures show you're hitting the mark consistently. Always go for more for the rest of your career as a stamp dealer. It's the way success is built.

If your advertising isn't working, the worst thing to do would be to cancel it. Advertising always works when it offers something prospective customers want, has competitive prices or services and is written and laid out effectively. Also remember that good advertising sometimes is almost counter-intuitive. For instance, "white space," which many small business owners consider to be "wasted space," actually draws attention to your ad by making it stand out and look easier and faster to read.

However, advertising isn't the only area that requires thought and planning. Everything associated with your business demands it. It's important to have not only plans for the coming year, but for several years in advance. The way a successful business is created is to have a clear picture of where you want to be and then to test different ways of getting there as you go along. Then you do more of what works, quit doing what doesn't and keep generating and trying new ideas.

Many people become stamp dealers to have more freedom and flexibility in their lives. Paradoxically, even a stamp dealer's spare time should be accounted for. I once astonished a dealer friend who asked me over the phone what I was doing. I replied that I was working on next year's mail-bid sale schedule and was refining the conditions of sale and my consignment contract.

He laughed and invited me to a sporting event. I declined with thanks, replying that I had already allocated the evening's time toward the task at hand and would gladly accompany him on another night if I were free of the business's responsibilities. I don't think he understood, but I do know which of us reaps the biggest profits year after year.

Just as important as planning and time management is budgeting. In fact, they go together for all successful businesses. If you choose to budget unrealistically, you may as well not budget at all and watch your dream swirl down the drain. Budgeting is actually financial planning.

In our planning example, we decided to acquire 30 consignors in the coming year. We didn't increase or decrease a budgeted amount of money, although we would have increased the size of one or more of our ads if necessary. Although a larger ad costs more money, we would not be increasing our advertising budget. Instead, we would be spending from the amount that we had originally budgeted for advertising.

Once we hit our annual allocated amount, we have reached our budget. If at year-end we have spent more than our predetermined amount, we will be in a deficit position relative to our budget. Spending less puts us in a surplus situation.

When we budget, we allocate certain percentages of actual or projected revenue toward every real or anticipated expense item. What's left from revenue after expenses is our profit. If we don't stick to our budget and keep track of our figures, our company can slip away from us before we realize what has happened.

On a piece of paper, write your projections of revenue and expenses, month by month, for the coming year. Leave room to record actual revenue and expenses in the next column at the end of each month.

Also, keep a running total for each revenue and expense category and adjust your operation as you go along. You may find, for example, that you've grossly underestimated the costs of advertising. By the same token, you may have overstated your office supplies expense. As you acquire each year's figures, you'll have more reliable information for the next year's budget.

If you're using a computer, programs like Microsoft Money and Quicken cost as little as $15 to $25 and do an excellent job of giving you useful reports and graphs any time you punch a button. They take a day or two to study and set up and pay back handsomely in the months to come.

Whichever way you keep track of your figures, let's consider a budget with total revenue of $140,000. Income is broken down into three sources: store, show and mail-order. It is important that you set specific goals for each income source and carefully project each expense.

Advertising – This probably will account for at least 5 percent of gross receipts, and even higher in some months. We might, for example, consider spending $8,400 a year against projected revenue of $140,000. That's $1,400 more than the $7,000 we would spend if we allotted 5 percent revenue. We hope the additional $1,400 will generate $28,000 additional revenue ($28,000 x 5 percent = $1,400). This will be money well spent if our strategy pays off. If we find as the year passes that we aren't generating $20 in revenue for each dollar spent on advertising, we'll have to make our advertising more effective or lower our profit goals.

The area that will call for your greatest attention will be your advertising investment. Cultivate a plan that works for you and stick with it despite what other dealers tell you. Your business is unique.

Just as dollars are ascribed to every budget category, also assign inches to your one-, three- and five-year advertising plans. For example, let's say you are in the weeklies to the tune of a couple of classifieds and at least a two-inch ad in every issue. Add to this whatever you spend for advertising in society monthlies like *The American Philatelist*.

The advantage of budgeting words and inches is to resist the temptation to cut back if advertising rates go up. If anything, we want to increase the size of our ads each year as our sales increase.

If you followed my earlier advice to "test" and "key" your ads, it should be clear to you which publications are pulling their weight. What you have to do is chart out your expenses per publication on a cost-per-word (classified) or per-column-inch (display) basis. Cut back advertising in publications that clearly are not helping attract business, and budget additional space in the newspapers and magazines whose ads are working for you.

Be careful not to let partial figures mislead you. If you get ten answers from one newspaper and two from another, you might be tempted to cut back on the one that produced only two. Those figures are called the front-end results. However, keep track of how much repeat business you get from each customer to see what the back-end figures look like. If the ten customers spend $738 with you during the next year and the two spend $1,847, your most profitable paper really is the one that produced fewer responses.

Never eliminate your advertising in any publication that has potential customers. You must be visible everywhere you reasonably can expect to do business. You just don't have to be charitable. Spend most of your money where it does you the most good.

General – Includes customer refunds, transportation and other small miscellaneous items. You could also include monthly bank fees on your checking account and merchant credit card account.

Office Supplies – Here is one area that you have quite a bit of control over. Do you really need fresh scratch paper, rather than using the backs of surplus price lists? Do you turn your file folders inside out and use them again instead of buying new ones? Do you shop for the best prices on your computer paper and printer ribbons?

Postage – To mail a single letter at the first-class rate is a bargain indeed when you consider the traveling and handling involved. For a stamp dealer, however, the cost can be backbreaking if one is mailing out, say, 2,000 or 3,000 pieces of mail at least four times a year as well as daily correspondence and order shipping. We might want to consider allocating 4 percent of our annual revenue to postage, or about $5,900.

When you consider that $4 out of every $100 sale goes to pay postage expenses, you can see why most dealers no longer pay all of the postage costs on an order. I recommend that you charge a minimum postage fee with every order, regardless of its size. These days, the going rate is $2 on smaller orders and as much as $4 or $5 on larger ones.

You may not want to charge that much, however. One reason is that normally the postage and mailing materials for a small purchase don't cost even $2, let alone $4, and your customers may see you as tacking on a hidden charge.

Printing – Keep your costs down by utilizing your computer and your quick printer. Your local quick printer can reduce your copy to fit the format of your pieces. You should also consider bulk mail for selected printing. (See the Chapter 6.)

Professional Fees – In this category we include subscriptions to the philatelic weeklies, dues for professional societies, and reference books. A reasonable budget might include $50 a month for these items. Just remember that most society and association fees are paid annually.

New Stock – I suggest spending at least half of your in-coming funds towards new stock acquisition. The more that you can spend, the better for your business. Throughout a year, and considering every type of purchase, you should be able to double your money. Thus the one-half recommendation.

Rent – Location is vitally important for a store. Try to keep this expense under 10 percent of revenue. I consider the fees I pay for show tables to be rent.

Telephone – It's advisable not to skimp here. Make those calls, sell those stamps and get those consignments. Just get into the habit of not talking about the weather or the latest sports score. You're making a business call, not a social call. Remember the distinction. Also take advantage of the evening, late-night and weekend rates whenever you can.

As your business grows, your weekly and monthly figures will become the tools with which you'll shape your long-range plans. Intelligent stamp dealers work with one-, three- and five-year plans. Most don't make much without clear future vision.

One long-range plan might include a 75 percent increase in sales volume five years down the road. Although it is an optimistic forecast, it is reasonable. With hard work, you might increase sales by 75 percent within three years.

By keeping expenses under tight control, it might be possible to hire a part-time employee next year. A $12,000 revenue jump affords you the luxury of paying somebody else to put the address labels on the envelopes, fold and stuff the price lists, run to the post office and the like. You can use the time that is freed for more profitable tasks.

It's also important that a long-range budget include realistic estimates for expenses. Coming increases in postage rates must be taken into consideration, and you also can anticipate price increases in printing, professional fees and telephone rates. If you're planning to undertake a more aggressive telemarketing plan than in years past, you can expect your telephone bill to increase accordingly.

What happens if sales exceed your wildest expectations? I recommend funneling the extra funds into advertising and building inventory to increase the size of your operation even further. The result will be a continued upward spiral of sales. Resist the temptation to pocket the surplus. Building your business is your constant and most-important goal.

As you become established you will want to refine your revenue budgeting. Keep the main income categories established in our earlier example, i.e., store, shows and mail-order. Add specific sub-categories to each source. Examples of sub-categories are 19th century unused, 19th century used, 20th century unused, 20th century used, postal history, philatelic supplies, philatelic literature, and back of the book. Your mail-order category also can be given a mail-bid sale sub-category to allow you to watch that revenue stream separately.

To a point, more detail will enhance your budget analysis and provide you with a better idea of those areas of your business that are losers or marginally profitable and those that are highly profitable.

Chapter 12
Welcome Colleague

Welcome! You are now a member of the happy trade known as stamp dealing. As in any group, there are ground rules. Some are written; some are traditional.

As a member of the American Stamp Dealers' Association, you will be expected to conduct your business ethically. As a dealer who wants to remain in business, your customers will expect you to provide outstanding service.

Always have high regard for the intelligence of *all* your clients. Always represent material accurately and treat your customers the way you would like to be treated. Dealers who knowingly do things like selling regummed stamps as having original gum or buying stamps for less than they know the stamps are worth, are quickly branded coast to coast as rip-off artists.

I earlier wrote about the two R's of successful stamp dealing: recognition and reputation. Recognition comes from your steady advertising. Reputation comes from your business practice. Your reputation, good or bad, will stick to you like glue. A bad reputation will harm your business in ways you never may know or will put you out of business quickly.

These are some of the unwritten rules of stamp dealing:
• Never put down another dealer in front of a collector. Dealers are just as talkative as collectors. When both groups get together, gab sessions can last hours. If, for example, the conversation turns to dealer Joe Schmo and his extra-fine stamps, which are no better than some other dealer's fine to very-fines, sensible dealers keep quiet.

Regardless of your own feelings towards Schmo and the quality of his grading proficiency, you risk your own reputation if you judge him behind his back. Your listeners know you'll judge them the same way when they aren't present. If you have clear evidence Joe is unethical, then by all means institute a formal complaint with the ASDA or American Philatelic Society. You help yourself and the hobby when you act to keep stamp dealing ethical.

• Never put down a dealer to another dealer. While talking on the phone to a colleague, the conversation can very easily shift gears without notice. Avoid any temptation to back-stab.

• Don't put down collectors. Saying Charlie Collector is stupid for collecting lawn bowling on stamps is saying part of the business that provides your living is stupid. Such comments reflect more on the intelligence of the speaker than on anyone else.

• Don't knowingly overprice. You've just purchased a vast holding of 19th century covers. In it you discover some pristine Columbian Exposition cards. Cleanliness is the rule here, and you realize you've got some high profit potential. The cards each depict a site on the fairgrounds. Although you know the going rate is $20 apiece, you consider pricing them at $39 each and justifying the higher price by describing the 100th anniversary of the Chicago Exposition and the 500th anniversary of Columbus' voyage to America.

However, think instead about the long-term good you can do for your reputation if you price each at $18—10 percent off your regular price. Still point out the historical significance, and also let your customer know this is a special opportunity because of a favorable purchase you made.

The result? You enhance your reputation. Your discounted selling price still affords you a slightly better-than-usual markup. Your customer is pleased and trades more with you, instead of with dealers who overprice. Your customer tells friends who also become your customers.

It is said that a satisfied customer tells three other people about his or her good experience. On the other hand, a dissatisfied customer tells nine others! When your customers discover they have paid $39 for $20 exposition cards, your short-term profits will turn into a long-term losses.

• Always grant a trade discount. There cannot be anything in your stock that is priced so close to cost as to preclude this courtesy. Dealers routinely give other dealers a 10 percent discount or more. I once found a lovely cover that I knew would sell at once to one of my customers. "How much?" I asked the dealer who owned it. Although the price was clearly marked, I expected anything but the answer I received: "Fifty dollars; the price is plainly marked." Having already identified myself as a dealer, I expected some courtesy discount.

Two years later I had the privilege of returning the favor when the same dealer visited my show table. His memory wasn't nearly as good as mine.

• Subscribe to philatelic publications. One indispensable publication for dealers is *The Stamp Wholesaler,* published every other week by Krause Publications, publisher of this book. *SW* is the world's largest stamp dealer periodical and the only one in North America. It is filled with trade news, how-to articles and other information you'll need to succeed in your business.

Its sister, *Stamp Collector* newspaper, is published weekly for hobbyists and is known for its following among the kinds of serious collectors dealers seek as customers. Write Krause Publications, 700 East State Street, Iola, WI 54990-0001, for subscription information.

There are many other philatelic newspapers, magazines and specialty journals. Read as many as possible. The difference between professional and amateur stamp dealers is knowledge. Your gains are likely to exceed by far the modest cost of the subscriptions.

So again, "Welcome colleague!" May your career be long and fruitful. And may you give to philately as much or more than you receive from it.